© Royal Garden Hotel 2015

ISBN 978-1-909811-28-7
A CIP catalogue record for this book is available from the British Library

Published by TriNorth Ltd
Design: Rob Whitehouse, TriNorth Ltd, www.trinorth.co.uk
Typeset in Avant Garde
Printed in Malta by 21six

CONTENTS

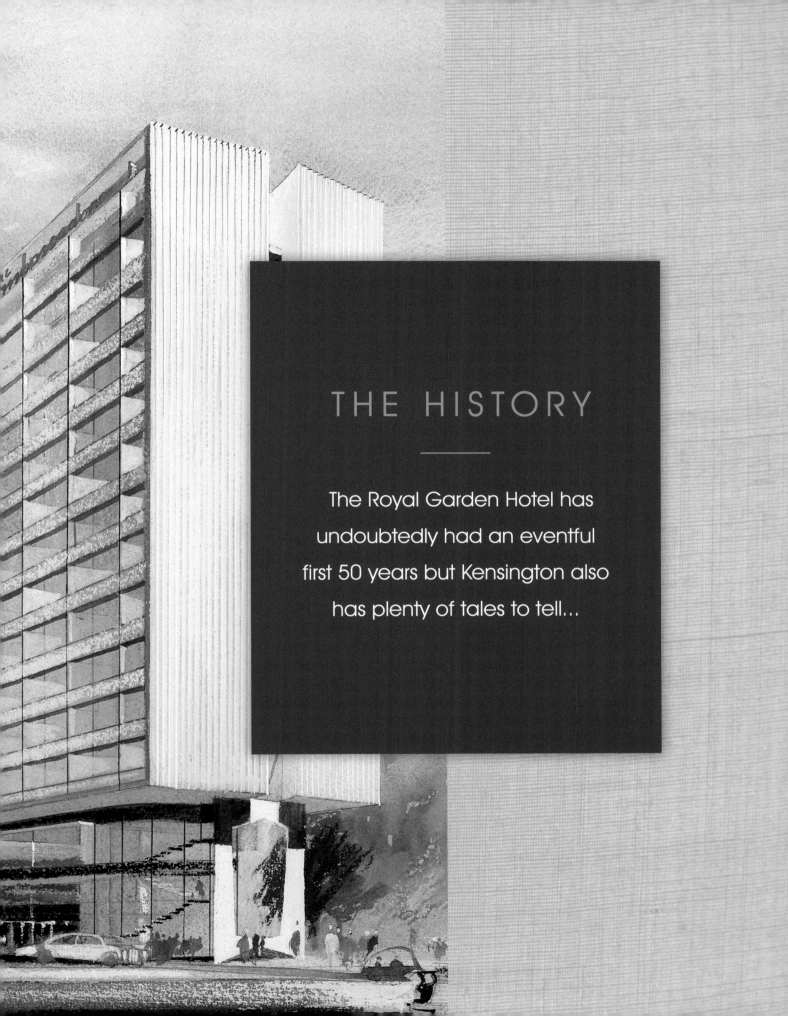

THE HISTORY

The Royal Garden Hotel has undoubtedly had an eventful first 50 years but Kensington also has plenty of tales to tell...

THE LIFE AND TIMES

The 50 years since the hotel threw open its doors in 1965 have seen considerable change. While we've had just the one monarch on the British throne for all of this time, we've witnessed a number of hugely significant historical and technological developments. We have witnessed man walk on the moon for the first time, the end of the Vietnam War, the Berlin Wall being torn down, and the birth of the Internet. We have seen nine US Presidents (Johnson, Nixon, Ford, Carter, Reagan, Bush, Clinton, Bush and Obama) and eight UK Prime Ministers (Wilson, Heath, Callaghan, Thatcher, Major, Blair, Brown and Cameron) as well.

But what was happening as the Royal Garden Hotel, which had been under construction since 1960 on the site of the former Royal Palace Hotel, welcomed its first guests back in the summer and autumn 1965? Well, the Hollies' *I'm Alive* hit number 1 in the charts, cigarette advertising on TV was banned, Mod and Rocker culture swept across the UK, Singapore announced its independence, *Thunderbirds* debuted on ITV, Bob Dylan "went electric", and The Beatles – the epitome of the Swinging Sixties – were in New York playing the first stadium concert in music history.

Such modern concerns were a world away from Kensington's ancient and medieval origins. The area was situated on the Great Western Road, one of the main original highways, built by the Romans and running from central London to Staines.

The first mention of Kensington appears in the Domesday Book, in 1086, under the Latin name of Chenesitone, a translation of the Anglo-Saxon Kenesignetun, meaning Kenesigne's meadows or land; although it may also derive from Chenesi Tun, meaning town of Chenesi's people (Chenesi being the colloquial name for Edward the Confessor).

Fast forward to the early 17th century, and Kensington had became popular with the elite because of its location near to London, and a reputation for clean and healthy air.

During this period, Kensington boasted a profusion of nurseries and was very fertile ground for flowers, vegetables and orchards.

The court of reigning monarchs William and Mary, escaping from the damp riverside air at Whitehall, arrived at Nottingham House (later known as Kensington Palace) in 1689 and the area started to be developed

"This Town standing in a wholesome Air, not above Three Miles from London, has ever been resorted to by Persons of Quality and Citizens, and for many Years past Honour'd with several fine Seats belonging to the Earls of Nottingham, Warwick, etc."

John Bowack, Antiquities of Middlesex, 1705.

in a way we would recognise it today. As noted by writer John Bowack, it was this move that precipitated Kensington's reputation.

From a map of 1741-45 by John Rocque, Kensington might be unrecognisable in its abundance of fields, meadows and orchards; but that was about to change as King William hired Christopher Wren to turn Nottingham House into an appropriate royal residence.

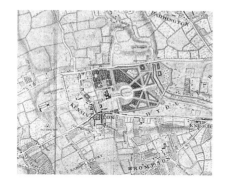

William's wife, Queen Mary, had the gardens developed although they were already renowned before that time; as far back as 1664, Samuel Pepys was attending events there.

"Since which time it has Flourish'd even almost beyond Belief, and There is also abundance of Shop-keepers, and all sort of Artificers in it, which make it appear rather like part of London, than a Country Village."

John Bowack, Antiquities of Middlesex, 1705.

The last King to be a permanent resident at the house was George II, whose wife Queen Caroline redesigned and extended the gardens between 1727 and 1754, getting rid of the formal gardens in front of the Palace and replacing them with informal parkland. She employed Charles Bridgeman, who created, among other things, the Serpentine and the Round Pond. Caroline also made it open to "respectably dressed people" and by the reign of William IV the gardens were opened to the public.

Following the death of Queen Caroline, the Palace was abandoned by the monarchs, and George III never lived there. It was renovated in the early 1800s and Queen Victoria was born there in 1819, calling it home until her accession in 1837. However its reputation was not re-established until Victoria opened it to the public at the end of the 19th century, by which time London was a very different city.

Before the 19th century there were few if any large hotels in London. British country landowners often lived in London for part of the year but usually rented a

The King's Arms Hotel on Kensington High Street in the 1880s. In the decade that followed, the Royal Palace Hotel took shape, followed some 70 years later by the Royal Garden Hotel on the same site.

The Empress Ballroom at the Royal Palace Hotel.

house if they did not own one, rather than staying in a hotel. Numbers of business and foreign visitors were very small by modern standards, with the accommodation available to them including Gentlemen's clubs, lodging houses and coaching inns.

A few more modern hotels were built in the early 19th century, such as Mivart's, the precursor to Claridge's, in 1812, but up to the mid-19th century, London hotels were generally small.

Then, as the trains started to bring many more short-term visitors to London, the railway companies took the lead in accommodating them by building a series of "railway hotels" near to their London termini. These companies, the largest businesses in the country at the time, built big status-symbol hotels like the Midland Grand Hotel at St Pancras (now the Renaissance), the Great Western Hotel at Paddington (now the Hilton), the Great Northern Hotel at King's Cross, the Great Eastern Hotel at Liverpool Street (now the Andaz), the Charing Cross Hotel, the Great Central Hotel at Marylebone (now The Landmark) and the Grosvenor Hotel at Victoria.

Away from the railway stations, The Langham Hotel was the largest hotel in the city when it opened in 1865, The Savoy (the first London hotel with en-suite bathrooms to every room) came into being in 1889, with Claridge's being rebuilt and The Ritz opening in the decade that followed.

At the same time, at the end of the 19th century, on the site of the present Royal Garden Hotel, emerged the Royal Palace Hotel. In 1800 Kensington had been home to fewer than 10,000 people; by 1901, that number had increased to 175,000. Part of the reason was that, in 1851, London had seen the Great Exhibition open in Hyde Park, with over six million visitors between May and October. Profits were partly used to buy 87 acres of land in Kensington and establish Albertopolis, the centre for Britain's artistic and scientific culture. To provide access to this area, the District and Metropolitan lines were extended west, so that by 1871 Kensington High Street was served by new railway routes, and Kensington underwent a period of rapid development.

The new hotel was a thing of wonder. The *Kensington News* of 23 July 1892 reported: "The hotel being erected on the site of the old King's Arms is to be opened in February, and the flat roof with which it is proposed to top it will command an unrivalled view of a London fog. Something is to be said, by the way, in favour of extending the Trade Mark system to the names of royal and public buildings and to other edifices which give a prestige to the neighbourhood in which they are situated."

The hotel contained over 300 rooms, had a spacious lounge and several private dining rooms. On the upper ground, known as the grand floor, there were reception rooms, a reading room, a general drawing room, dining room, coffee room, ladies' drawing room and a music room, all with views over Kensington Gardens. That flat roof was for promenading and acted as a smoking lounge. The Empress Ballroom, "a marvel of beauty, elegance and convenience", with its own entrance onto Kensington High Street, was later opened, adding a further level of luxury to the hotel.

Drawings illustrating external and internal views of the Royal Palace Hotel.

The Royal Palace Hotel,

Kensington, London, W.

SITUATED on the Western side of Kensington Gardens, directly overlooking the grounds of Kensington Palace (the birthplace of Queen Victoria) with its entrance in High Street, the Royal Palace Hotel enjoys the advantages of a position unequalled in London. Built on a district always famous for its open spaces, its fine air, and its deep red gravel soil, it commands extensive views of Kensington Gardens and Hyde Park, and is within a few minutes of the centre of London. High Street Station for the Metropolitan and District Railways, Piccadilly and Bakerloo Tubes, Queen's Road Station for the Central London Tube, are but a minute's walk from the Hotel. Omnibuses for all parts of London and Suburbs pass the door. The Albert Hall, South Kensington Museums, Imperial Institute, Earl's Court Exhibition, and Olympia are within walking distance.

ROYAL PALACE HOTEL, LONDON, W.

Bedroom.

ROYAL PALACE HOTEL, LONDON, W.

A Corner in the Drawing Room.

Royal Palace Hotel, London, W.

Public Reception Rooms.

The Public Reception Rooms are the most luxurious and comfortable in London. The handsome Salle à Manger with its separate tables, the Reading Room and Library, the elegant Ladies' Drawing Room, the Billiard Room, &c., all overlook the Park. There is also a Moorish Lounge, and a Coffee Room for dinners à la carte.

Bedrooms.

						per day.
Single Bed Rooms	-	-	-	-	-	from 4/6
Double Bed Rooms	-	-	-	-	-	„ 7/-
Bed Room & Dressing Room	-	-	-	-	-	„ 8/6
Sitting Room & Bed Room	-	-	-	-	-	„ 17/-
Bed Room & Sitting Room, with Bath Room & Dressing Room, en Suite	-	-	-	-	-	„ 22/6
Visitors Servants' Bedrooms	-	-	-	-	-	„ 2/6

No Charge is made for Lights or Attendance.

Suites of Rooms.

In addition to a large number of luxuriously furnished double and single bedrooms, there are a considerable number of self-contained suites of private

The Ball Room,

As the 20th century progressed, the upper end of the London hotel business flourished, especially between the two World Wars, with many land-owning families no longer able to maintain a London house and therefore staying at hotels instead. There was also an increasing number of foreign visitors, especially Americans, leading to the opening of the Grosvenor House Hotel and the Dorchester around 1930.

After World War II, hotel construction slowed dramatically, and consequently the government offered grants to kickstart the industry. The London Hilton on Park Lane opened in 1963 and the Palace Hotel was completely demolished, paving the way for the construction of the Royal Garden Hotel, rebuilt under the design of Colonel Richard Seifert and coming under the Oddeninos Hotel Group banner.

An artist's impression from 1960 of the then unnamed project by architects R. Seifert & Partners. The notes say: "A 400-room project still in the planning application stage, for a site near the entrance to Kensington Palace Gardens. The ground floor will be given over largely to shops, displacing the reception area to the first, which will also have restaurant and banqueting rooms; second-floor roof-garden above restaurant."

The hotel under construction and being completed, from 1962 to 1965.

A HOTEL IS BORN

The project, which meant four years of construction on the High Street, was deemed viable as air travel and tourism became the norm. The number of overseas visitors to London grew from 1.6 million in 1963 to 6 million in 1974, with a vibrant music and fashion scene making London *the* place to visit. The hotel threw open its doors in 1965 and very soon became a venue where people wanted to be seen.

THE PLACE TO BE

The hotel became a magnet for both locals and travellers. Its four restaurants ensured there was something for everyone and its association with England winning the World Cup meant that it very rapidly built up a loyal following. Kensington was right at the heart of the Swinging Sixties scene – an incredibly exciting place to be with trendy shops and great music everywhere.

As well as The Monkees, Paul McCartney and a host of other stars popping in, Biba came into being in 1964 when fashion designer Barbara Hulanicki opened a small dress shop. So successful was it (Hulanicki sold her entire stock in the first hour of trading and young girls travelled from all over the country, queuing for hours to get into Biba) that it had to move to larger premises within two years, this time a grocer's shop in Church Street. Biba had to move again in 1969, into where Whole Foods is situated today, as a department store selling clothes, jewellery and household goods.

Royal Garden Hotel
LONDON, W8

WESTERN 8000   TELEX 261214   T.A. ROYGARTEL, LONDON

TARIFF

Rates per day

	MIN	MED	MAX
Single Room	4gns	5gns	5½gns
Double or Twin-Bedded Room	7gns	8½gns	9½gns
Suites from	13½gns		

All rooms have private bath, shower, television, radio, direct-dial telephone and electronic message system.

The minimum rate applies only between Oct. 31st—April 1st.

Continental Breakfast	7/6
English Breakfast	12/6
Table d'Hote Luncheon	25/–
Table d'Hote Dinner	35/–

A 10% service charge will be added to all accounts to cover staff gratuities.

AN ODDENINO ENTERPRISE

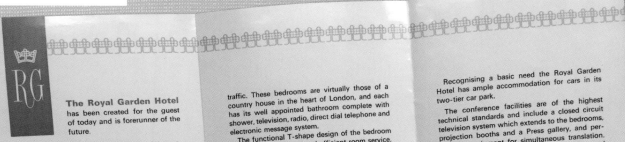

RG

The Royal Garden Hotel has been created for the guest of today and is forerunner of the future.

It has all the comforts and amenities of the out-moded "de luxe" hotel but has been streamlined for contemporary living. Nevertheless, it is intended to maintain the British traditions of courtesy and personal service.

The location of the Hotel reflects the westward flow of London's present-day activities. It is beautifully situated in Kensington Gardens, adjoining Kensington Palace, and is unique in that all the double rooms, which have sliding glass picture windows opening on to generous balconies, have an uninterrupted vista of parkland which is not divided by a road bearing heavy traffic. These bedrooms are virtually those of a country house in the heart of London, and each has its well appointed bathroom complete with shower, television, radio, direct dial telephone and electronic message system.

The functional T-shape design of the bedroom floors ensures speedy and efficient room service.

The four restaurants provide every type of food and service, at times and prices which fit all circumstances.

The Maze Coffee House operates on a 24-hour basis, providing coffee and light meals in an informal atmosphere with recorded music.

The Bulldog Grill provides food as British as the name denotes, and from the adjoining Bulldog Bar, all types of famous British draught beers are available.

The Garden Room serves international food and exceptional wines in the elegant way which has made **Oddenino's** world famous, finally . . .

The Royal Roof is a luxurious restaurant with soft music and a sophisticated ambiance. Its breathtaking views of London after dark, make it an ideal rendezvous for late diners and theatre-goers.

Recognising a basic need the Royal Garden Hotel has ample accommodation for cars in its two-tier car park.

The conference facilities are of the highest technical standards and include a closed circuit television system which extends to the bedrooms, projection booths and a Press gallery, and permanent equipment for simultaneous translation. The Palace Suite accommodates one thousand people in its pillar free area and can be divided by a lead impregnated curtain which renders each room completely soundproof.

The flexible banqueting arrangements permit a party as small as four in number to be held in a private dining room, and can cater for as many as five hundred and fifty at a formal dinner.

Whether occupying a single room or the penthouse suite with its 50 feet living room, three double bedrooms and bathrooms and its fabulous view, every guest at the **Royal Garden Hotel** enjoys the same amenities and services which make this Hotel unique in the United Kingdom.

There are forty elegantly furnished suites with balconies, and butler service is available if required.

AN ODDENINO ENTERPRISE

CAPTURING THE MARKET

A succession of Senior and General Managers came and went as the hotel found its niche, adapting to changing markets and looking to benefit from the increase in visitors from all parts of the world and also from the corporate market. As James Brown, General Manager from 1975-91 says: "We had a huge number of rooms but also the banqueting space to go with it, which broadened the spectrum of business of the hotel. There was the banking market, the pharmaceutical market, the corporate market, the North American incentive market, and then the leisure market – and we could cater for them all. Take the incentive market – what was great was you could allocate 200 rooms and have a banqueting space for a welcome party or a cocktail party or dinner."

People don't come back to the Royal Garden *just* for the fun of it

They like our serious side, too. Perhaps we tend to be a bit serious when it comes to their comfort and enjoyment, but we do feel these things are rather important.

Whichever of our five hundred rooms they stay in, they'll have their own bath, shower, radio, television and direct-dial telephone.

In our restaurants they'll be pampered and served some of the finest cuisine in London; in our Royal Roof, a fabulous late-night rendezvous on the 10th floor, they can dine and dance until the early hours.

Next time *you're* coming to London, stay at the Royal Garden and make your visit all the more enjoyable.

Royal Garden Hotel
London W8 4PT   Telephone: 01-937 8000

Oddenino's London Hotels:
ROYAL GARDEN · THE WHITE HOUSE · ATHENAEUM COURT · ALEXANDRA NATIONAL

The Banqueting Room in the late 1960s.

Now they tell me! For the same money I could have held this convention in London *and* at the Royal Garden Hotel

Many American companies have proved that it costs no more to fly to London and hold a convention than it does to travel across the States to a venue. But cost isn't the only thing.

Oddenino's Royal Garden is one of London's newest hotels and has been specifically designed to handle international conferences. Its largest suite comfortably accommodates nine hundred and is equipped with all essential facilities, including closed-circuit television, projection booths, telex, press gallery and simultaneous translation system.

A team of experts is always on hand to advise, assist and ensure the smooth running of all types of function.

The hotel has over five hundred rooms and suites, all equipped with private bath, shower, radio, television and direct-dial telephone. The cuisine at the Royal Garden is truly outstanding.

For relaxation after the day's business is done, there are the hotel bars and three restaurants. One of these, on the tenth floor, is an elegant and luxurious night spot, open for dining and dancing until the early hours.

London's theatres and West End entertainment centres are only minutes away and the hotel will gladly arrange special group visits on request.

For further information, please contact Michael Clayton, Sales Manager, Royal Garden Hotel, London, W.8, or Leonard Hicks Organisation, 1345 Avenue of the Americas, New York, N.Y. 10019. Telephone 765 6770.

CONFERENCE ORGANISER

ODDENINO'S
Royal Garden
Hotel
London

THE CHANGING FACE

The hotel did not stand still, of course, and modernisation and refurbishment have been constant themes throughout its existence, whether taking out the balconies; closing and opening restaurants, bars and coffee shops; and upgrading rooms (the hotel had almost 500 when it opened and 394 today). It became part of the Rank Organisation in the early 1970s, and saw a huge number of Middle Eastern guests coming to stay around halfway through the decade, an annual influx that continues to this day. A four-year renovation programme, started in 1982 and completed as the hotel celebrated its 20th anniversary, saw the arrival of more elegant, spacious bedrooms, the décor and layout of public areas being refreshed and the Gallery Bar (now Bertie's Bar) coming into being. Brown says: "Everyone understood we had to maintain the hotel's reputation. Staff turnover in the hotel business is traditionally high but we managed to slow that trend down quite considerably by taking the word "no" out of the vocabulary. You can spend millions on refurbishing hotels but at the end of the day you're only as good as your staff."

A NEW ERA

In the early 1990s, the Goodwood Group of Hotels, which owns the Goodwood Park and the York Hotel in Singapore, was looking for hotel investments in London. After evaluating a number of possibilities, The Chairman, the late Tan Sri Khoo Teck Puat (right), was delighted to settle on the Royal Garden Hotel.

At that time the hotel, which was owned by The Rank Organisation, was closed and undergoing a major programme of structural and cosmetic renovation. Once this was completed, the hotel reopened in April 1996, under the Goodwood Group of Hotels' ownership.

ROYAL GARDEN HOTEL

The staff gather as the hotel reopens in 1996.

With new General Manager Graham Bamford (right) at the helm, together with a brand new executive team, many of whom are still here today, the hotel was gearing up for the 21st century.

Over the last 20 years, the Royal Garden has continued to undergo many changes. In 2008 the hotel opened Min Jiang on the tenth floor. The concept was modelled on the successful Min Jiang restaurants that the Goodwood Group operates in Singapore. Min Jiang London has received critical acclaim and has now established itself as a destination restaurant.

Then came a rolling £45 million refurbishment programme which was completed in Spring 2012 in

time for the London Olympics, with all the bedrooms, public areas and conference and event facilities being updated. The Park Terrace restaurant also had a major facelift to provide a modern, stylish environment for hotel guests to enjoy an all-day dining experience and finally, the main kitchen was fully refurbished in 2014.

The Royal Garden Hotel is now perfectly attuned to modern living and travel, and keeps the family-friendly ethos at the heart of everything it does.

ENTERTAINMENT

Joan Collins, Dustin Hoffman, Justin Bieber to name but three – the Royal Garden Hotel has always attracted some of the most famous celebrities on the planet.

Here are their stories

THE HIGH LIFE

There's always been something alluring about the very best hotels. The promise of celebrity, the ghosts of film and music stars who have graced their lifts, corridors and bedrooms; the hotel is their hideaway when selling out stadiums or filming movies.

As celebrated American author and journalist Joan Didion says, the top hotels become as much a part of a cultural movement as a song or film, and the Royal Garden is no different. When the hotel opened its doors in 1965, Kensington was at the centre of a revolution in London. Post-war austerity was fading, and young people were in search of a good time, determined to make the 1960s *their* decade. And, boy, did they manage that, making London the centre of the cultural universe, bringing with them long hair, a sense of freedom, glamour and, above all, the love of a good party.

"Great hotels have always been social ideas, flawless mirrors to the particular societies they service"
Joan Didion

HEY, CAN I HAVE MY HAT BACK?

Royal Garden Doorman, John Sweeney, was the loser when international star Bob Dylan "borrowed" his top hat for his Blackbushe Concert. Dylan stayed at the Royal Garden while in the U.K. for both of his sell-out concerts. He took a fancy to John Sweeney's hat, borrowed it – and liked it so much he took it back to the USA. John is now wearing an old hat until his new hat, which is on order, is delivered. Never mind – he knows his hat is keeping good company as can be seen in this photograph of Dylan wearing the famous hat which, incidentally, costs £76.00 to replace!

Actor Quentin Crisp is seen with impresario Peter Cotes at a dinner given in his honour in the Gloucester prior to his departure on an extensive

The Royal Garden Hotel became synonymous with swinging 1960s London. The coolest musicians from both sides of the Atlantic saw the Royal Garden as the go-to hotel, with the likes of Frank Zappa, The Monkees, The Beatles, Chuck Berry, Tammy Wynette, Petula Clark, The Eagles, Mick Jagger, Rod Stewart, Johnny Cash and Sonny and Cher, who took over the Royal Suite, becoming part of the hotel's folklore as the good times stretched into the 1970s. Bob Dylan even borrowed Royal Garden doorman John Sweeney's hat for a concert – and then took it back to the USA with him!

Bands came from Europe too, with ABBA, the most popular band in the UK at the time, checking into the hotel. The Royal Garden also embraced the cheesier side of music, hosting a champagne party for the 1968 Eurovision Song Contest, which was won by Spain (Cliff Richard came in second with *Congratulations*).

It wasn't just musicians in flares, tie-dye and hairbands who made the hotel their London home. The world's hottest actors such as Dustin

Hoffman, Richard Attenborough, Glenn Ford, Telly Savalas, Oliver Reed, Claudia Cardinale, Charlotte Rampling and Kirk Douglas would command a room of reporters and journalists, as the hotel was often used for press conferences and photo shoots to promote their films.

Of course, with rock 'n' roll celebrities, you get a few controversial moments. It's expected; it goes with the territory. Youth, fame and ego is a cocktail to ensure the diligent Royal Garden staff were often on their toes when a famous name was in town. Usually, all was quiet, but sometimes, just occasionally, there were a few more challenging guests to look after. Although the Royal Garden Hotel was never witness to anything as extreme as The Who's Keith Moon driving his car through the glass doors of the entrance to ask for the keys to his room, or Led Zeppelin riding their Harley-Davidsons through the corridors, it has been witness to drama with The Mamas & The Papas – of *California Dreamin'* fame.

As the lustre of the 1960s and early 1970s started to wear off in London, the Royal Garden Hotel kept the capital swinging and never stopped welcoming famous guests. In the 1980s it became one of the go-to places for film première parties, with stars such as Michael Caine and Joan Collins leading huge entourages from movie screenings to dance the night away. Hollywood icon Paul Newman also stopped by to promote his film *The Color of Money* at the hotel in 1987.

Entertainers such as Mike Yarwood were long-term guests, while fellow comedians Bruce Forsyth, Jimmy Tarbuck, Bob Monkhouse and Les Dawson also found the hotel to their liking.

As musical fashions changed, so did the celebrity hotel guests. Plenty of jazz, soul, gospel and blues singers and musicians picked the Royal Garden as their hotel-of-choice in the 1980s – including Mavis Staples, The Cars, Bobby Womack, Billy Joel, the Osmonds, Mick Fleetwood, David Essex, The Temptations and Tom Browne. English popstar Boy George also held a press reception here at the height of his fame in 1984.

It remains a perfect location for music stars, with its close proximity to the Royal Albert Hall, Shepherd's Bush Empire and Hammersmith Apollo ensuring the hotel attracts world-famous stars from all across the musical spectrum, from opera singers to Meat Loaf to Elton John to My Chemical Romance to Tom Petty and Neil Young.

And it's not just old-school legends who choose the Royal Garden Hotel, but also the biggest pop-stars on the planet. Michael Jackson stayed here, as did One Direction and Rihanna, and in 2012, the hotel was surrounded by screaming teenage girls in scenes not witnessed since the days of Beatlemania as Justin Bieber checked in for a memorable stay.

Facing page, top to bottom: Paul McCartney; Bob Dylan; Paul Newman. This page: Mavis Staples; Joan Collins with General Manager James Brown; Ric Ocasek of the Cars.

Of course, it's not just actors and musicians who can entertain. Entrepreneur Richard Branson is a fan of the hotel and even took Royal Garden pillows with him on his attempt to circumnavigate the Earth in a hot-air balloon in 1998.

The Royal Garden Hotel is also proud of creating its own entertainment. John Wilson is a world-famous conductor and arranger who leads his own orchestra. He's played at the Proms and all over the world, but it all started at the Royal Garden Hotel with a decade-long residence which charmed hotel guests. His brilliance quickly spread by word of mouth and brought in many of the biggest and greatest names from the world of classical music.

The hotel also has strong links with the Royal College of Music, which brings through the next generation of classical music artists. And last but not least, since 2000 the hotel has played host to the International Live Music Conference, which attracts the biggest movers and shakers in the music industry from all around the world.

Despite the number of celebrities who have walked through the Royal Garden's entrance, the hotel has always been, and always will be, about the guests. So, over the next 20 pages, not only will you hear from some of the superstars who choose the Royal Garden Hotel as their preferred hotel, but also from guests who have bumped into celebrities in the corridors, lifts and restaurants. Some arrive at the hotel expecting to see a famous face during their stay, others dine at the restaurants for a dash of celeb-spotting, and few leave disappointed. They tell their stories too.

So, from The Monkees to Bieber, enjoy 50 years of entertainment at the Royal Garden Hotel!

This page, top to bottom: Richard Branson; the Osmonds; a photocall for the classical Brits; stars including Emma Thompson, Derek Jacobi, Kenneth Branagh, Alan Rickman and Dame Judi Dench gather for a charity function.

BIEBERMANIA

—— **Rooms Division Manager Patrick de la Mar remembers a time when everything went a little bit crazy.**

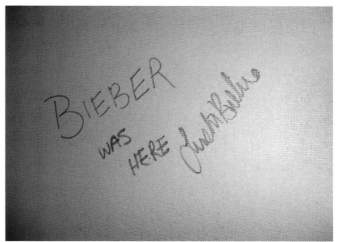

Justin Bieber stayed from 23-27 April 2012 in room 836. His arrival was chaotic as it was leaked on social media that he was coming to stay here with us. He was on a promotional tour so we believe the leak may have come from his management, but it was fun chaos rather than bad chaos! There were hundreds of screaming girls trying to get a glimpse when he arrived, and this intensified when he was inside the hotel.

Our main number was mentioned on Twitter and suddenly we were taking thousands of calls. Normally we take 1,000 in a day but on that day we took over 6,000, and we had nearly 20,000 calls in the four days he was with us – meaning we had around 15,000 people claiming they were Bieber's mum or his girlfriend Selena Gomez or just screaming as soon as we picked up the phone!

He wrote "Bieber was here" with a black marker pen on the wall in his hotel room. We temporarily covered this with a large picture and subsequently re-papered the wall. I believe Bieber's management company picked up the bill for it, but we paid for the trashed plants and flowers outside the hotel as well extra 24-hour security!

While it was hard work at the time and we had a few complaints from some guests (we were running a full hotel), having celebrity guests like Justin Bieber is exciting for the hotel, and something we've always had in our 50-year history. It's not only great publicity and shows how well respected the hotel is, but it's always a great morale-booster for the staff!

LIFE-CHANGER
—— Pauline Bird relates the extraordinary tale of her time with Frank Zappa.

It was August 1967, and I was working for the Forum Secretarial Agency. We worked in a lot of top hotels like the Dorchester, Grosvenor House and the newly opened Royal Garden Hotel. I normally worked for businessmen but was quite used to working with famous faces such as Gregory Peck, Douglas Fairbanks Jnr and Terence Rattigan.

I was sent along to the Royal Garden Hotel for a new client, Frank Zappa. I hadn't heard of him – I wasn't all that au fait with rock and roll at the time – and when I knocked on the door it was opened by a man dressed in a pink t-shirt and orange trousers, with his hair right down to his nipples. He looked like Charles II – there just wasn't anyone who looked like him at the time, and I thought I'd gone to the wrong room. But he said in his quiet drawl: "Pauline, come on in."

He had a suite and when I walked in there were all these guys hanging over sofas and chairs, wearing bright colours of purple, velvet and silk patterns. I was a model at the time as well, so I was stylishly but professionally dressed so I stuck out a bit. I said hello to the room but they were all bored to tears and looked past me. I went into the bedroom with Frank and sat at the desk and took out the little portable typewriter I had to take down these lyrics. But I couldn't use the typewriter, so I took them down in shorthand and told him I'd type them out in the office the next day and show it to him – it gave me the chance to see him again, as I was totally beguiled.

It was his first promotional trip to the UK ahead of concerts planned for a few months later. I had to take down the lyrics of *Absolutely Free*, which was his second album. The lyrics were to be printed in the *International Times*, which was a left-wing free newspaper at the time. I honestly could not understand some of the lyrics so I made them up – but instead of being cross with me he thought it was a hoot. He told me I should be writing my own lyrics because he thought they were hilarious. I told him if I did write my own lyrics I'd make them less rude!

The man was so completely different to his lyrics – he was calm, quiet, well-spoken, polite and very conservative. It was 1967 and men didn't listen to women at the time, we were treated like dolly birds. But this man actually engaged me in conversation and debated with me – that's what knocked me out about him.

After we'd finished the work he asked: "How would you like to be my date?" So we went to a speakeasy, this guy came through the crowd and Frank said: "Pauline, this is Eric Clapton." And I leant across and said: "And what do you play?" I had no idea who he was! I was so embarrassed.

A few months later, I met Frank again when they came back for the concert. I didn't know if he'd remember me but I went to the stage door and he immediately latched onto me when he saw me. He took me back to the Royal Garden Hotel, where they were staying again. There were all these people there after the concert, and musicians such as Jeff Beck were also there. It was wonderful fun.

A few months later I went to America to visit my sister and I met up with Frank, and he said he was going to write a book in California and he asked me to come out there with him to type it up. So I went out there to live with him, his wife and his band, and stayed for four years!

I came back to England after living with him and went to Cambridge University, and rarely spoke about my four years with Frank until I published my book about him in 2011 – *Freak Out! My Life With Frank Zappa*. I did much of my publicity for the book at the Royal Garden, and it was wonderful to be back at the place which completely changed my life in 1967.

MEETING FRIENDS IN THE LIFT

—— **Hotel guest Andy Mitchell on running into the 'Friends' star.**

I started staying regularly at the Royal Garden Hotel three or four years ago, and whenever my wife and I stay we say to each other: "I wonder if any celebs will be in this time?"

We spent the afternoon shopping and arrived back with our bags and got into the lift nearest the restaurant. We were joined by a lady and a gentleman, who said hello to me and smiled as they saw the size of the bags we had.

They left the floor before us, and I said to my wife: "I can't believe you didn't say hello!" She looked inquisitive and said she couldn't really see their faces because of the bag I had. Her face was a picture when I told her she had been stood next to one of the stars of her favourite TV show: Matt LeBlanc from *Friends*! Apparently my fault she hadn't seen him!

The following week I was down at the Royal Garden again. This time I was with some people from work and I was having a drink in Bertie's relaying the LeBlanc story before nipping up to my room to have a shower before dinner. I used the same lift, and this time I was joined by a man, a lady and a young guy. When I got back to my colleagues you can imagine the ridicule when I told them that this time in the lift it was Chris de Burgh and his family! I'm not sure to this day if they believe me!

SOUL LEGEND

—— **Bobby Womack was appearing in London when he checked in at the Royal Garden in 1988.**

Womack, who sadly died in June 2015 and was a regular visitor to the hotel up until his death, was inducted into the Rock and Roll Hall of Fame in 2009 after a career that spanned six decades. After a series of hits in the 1960s, and playing with the likes of Sam Cooke, Aretha Franklin and Ray Charles, he enjoyed a resurgence in the 1980s after releasing the R&B hit *If You Think You're Lonely Now* in 1981.

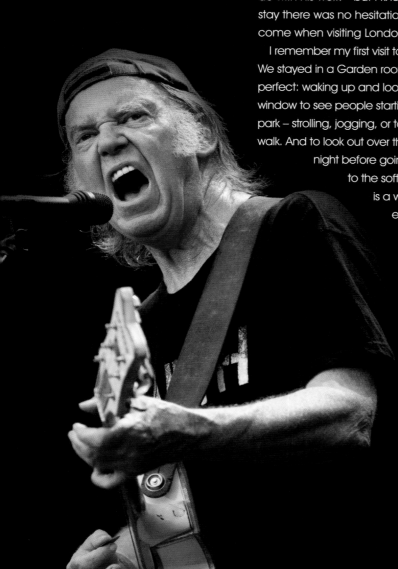

BUMPING INTO YOUR HERO

── Hotel guest Kerstin Perlkvist on a tease come true!

The Royal Garden hotel has been an important place for me and my husband Jan for many years. I'm not sure why my husband stayed there for the first time – something to do with his work – but I know that after that stay there was no hesitation about where to come when visiting London from Sweden.

I remember my first visit to the Royal Garden. We stayed in a Garden room and it was perfect: waking up and looking out of the window to see people starting their day in the park – strolling, jogging, or taking their dogs for a walk. And to look out over the skyline in the dark night before going to bed, listening to the soft music on the radio is a wonderful way to end the day.

We have stayed many times at the hotel, and the most memorable visit was last summer. Jan loves music and his favourite artist is Neil Young. So when Jan saw that Young was performing in Hyde Park last summer, he hurried to buy tickets and then told me: "We're going to London to hear Neil Young!" Luckily, I didn't take much persuading.

We came to London a few days before the concert. As usual we had a great time, and I was teasing my husband by telling him I was sure Neil Young would also be staying at the Royal Garden Hotel as it is so close to Hyde Park. Of course, I didn't really believe it for a minute as London has so many hotels!

On the day of the concert we returned to the hotel after a walk, and we were heading towards the lifts when a group of people came out from one of them. I almost walked into them and gave them a quick look. One of them looked very familiar…

My husband was behind me and I turned round and said: "Did you see?"

"No, what?" he answered. "That must have been Neil Young," I said. So Jan followed the group of people to see for himself. He came back a few minutes later with a happy smile on his face and confirmed that it really was Neil Young!

Later that afternoon we saw the other members of his band in the lobby, and Jan was able to recognise them all. The concert was fantastic and the opportunity to see him off stage made the experience all the sweeter.

THE MONKEES INVASION
—— The chart-topping sensations arrived at the Royal Garden Hotel for a press conference in 1967.

With hundreds of screaming fans outside, and 200 journalists inside, the Royal Garden Hotel welcomed the biggest pop act on the planet in 1967.

With their own comedy TV show, and a series of musical hits, The Monkees were hot property when they toured England for the first time in June of that year. At the time their records were selling more than The Beatles and The Rolling Stones combined.

After being met at Heathrow Airport by an army of girls, they caused mayhem when they later appeared on balconies at the Royal Garden to wave to the huge crowds below them.

They didn't have it all their own way, though. They drew heavy criticism from the musical press, who called them the "pre-Fab Four" in reference to their birth as a manufactured band for a TV show about an imaginary band who dreamed of being The Beatles… before fiction became reality when they started releasing records. They'd just released their third album, *Headquarters*, which was the first written by the band themselves rather than a team of producers, but they still received accusations of not playing all of their own instruments on the record.

However, they were warmly received at the Royal Garden Hotel for the press conference, with Americans Mike Nesmith, Peter Tork and Micky Dolenz and Englishman Davy Jones charming the packed room of reporters and photographers.

ORCHESTRAL MANOEUVRES IN THE PARK

—— **The world-renowned composer John Wilson talks about his decade-long residency at the Royal Garden Hotel with his own orchestra.**

I'd been out of the Royal College of Music for about a year, and my orchestra was playing at Chewton Glen Hotel. The orchestra was made up of my fellow students, so we were all very young.

I remember two things about one special evening. Ted Heath, the former Prime Minister, was there – he'd been wandering around and I glanced up into the audience and suddenly registered a Prime Minister was there! The

Manhattan Nights
at the Tenth.

second thing was meeting Graham Bamford, the General Manager at the Royal Garden. He approached me to ask if I'd like to have a look around the hotel, as he'd been listening to an orchestra who'd played there in the 1970s and was keen to bring that back.

We started with a one-off trial in 1996, and we ended up having a residency there for nine years! We were contracted to play once a month, but we'd often play more regularly if it was particularly busy or if we were wanted for private functions.

Graham gave us free rein – he knew we'd come up with the goods. He was so supportive. For us it was a great opportunity to get plenty of experience playing, and I always regard that residency as being the cornerstone that the orchestra's future was founded on. We built up our repertoire, and got to know the little fundamental things like what to wear, how to present yourself to the public and how to behave professionally.

The acoustics were good, and the atmosphere was wonderful. We were up on the 10th floor and it felt like you were in your own little world. All 22 of us would emerge from this tiny broom cupboard where we got changed into this amazing setting. And people would keep coming back to watch us at Manhattan Nights – and many of them still come to see us to this day.

For the last few years people seemed to want to dance more, so we brought in more saxophonists and used fewer strings. Some of the greatest musicians and players played in the orchestra across those nine years. Don Lusher, a world-famous trombonist who played for Frank Sinatra and Ella Fitzgerald, played with us. Sir Thomas Allen, the baritone, came for dinner one night and he sang a song with us. So there were all sorts of people like that who came to do guest spots, and that all came through word of mouth. They knew we were playing and they would just turn up.

Without Graham and the hotel I don't think the orchestra would be where it is today, which is in a pretty exalted position with invitations to play the Proms, performing at the Royal Albert Hall and record contracts and all of that. The hotel certainly played a really big part in us achieving that.

A SPOT OF BOTHER...
—— The hotel gets embroiled in controversy with The Mamas & The Papas.

With so many rock 'n' roll guests staying at the Royal Garden Hotel over its 50 years, it's inevitable that there will have been a spot of controversy at some point.

The first incident came two years after the hotel opened, and it involved American group The Mamas & The Papas, famous for their 1966 hit *California Dreamin'*.

When they docked at Southampton in October 1967, ahead of a concert at the Royal Albert Hall and a tour of Europe, band member Cass Elliot was immediately arrested for allegedly stealing keys and hotel blankets from the hotel after staying there the previous February.

She spent a night in custody and the charges were dropped the following morning at West London Magistrates Court. However, the hotel had been far more interested in settling a large unpaid bill left by Elliot than a key and some blankets, while the police were more interested in talking to Pic Dawson, who had been entrusted with the bill, because they suspected he was a drug trafficker.

After Elliot was acquitted, The Mamas & The Papas cancelled their shows and all scheduled television appearances and they briefly split up.

MOTOWN MASTERS
— **The Temptations enjoyed a resurgence in popularity while staying at the Royal Garden Hotel.**

One of the most influential Motown groups, The Temptations scored a succession of hits in the 1960s, including *My Girl*. They enjoyed a revival in the 1980s, and in 1986 they were promoting their smash *Lady Soul* when they stayed at the hotel.

Otis Williams, standing on the left, is the only original member of the band still performing live. Allie-Ollie Woodson, right, joined in 1984 as the public latched back on to The Temptations, while Richard Street, middle, joined in 1968.

CANDID CAMERA

— **Michael Putland, one of the world's most famous music photographers, on a damp start and snapping stars at the hotel.**

I first started in photography in 1963 when I was 16, straight out of school. The first company I worked for as an assistant had the photography contract for the Royal Garden Hotel when it opened.

I didn't come from a background that took me to posh hotels, so it was all very different for me, and I thought that the hotel was a bit special. One of the first shoots I did there was of the restaurant, using a few models. I think it was just before it opened, and in those days we had to set everything up with wires – all the lights used flash and they used these very, very large bulbs that if they went off in your hand would really damage it quite badly. So it took hours to fix this shoot up, and it was just starting to get dark when suddenly there was this huge crash of thunder and a flash of lightning, and the ceiling fell in! The

rain was pouring down on the inside of the window, flooding the carpets and we were running around picking up the lights to save them from being damaged – they were very expensive in those days. In the end we didn't even get the shot!

My first big music job at the hotel was in 1967, when I shot The Monkees when I went along to their press conference. I was just getting to know PRs in the music industry and getting myself into that scene, and it was an incredibly exciting time for me at the end of the swinging '60s. In case my memory was playing tricks about The Monkees, I checked on the internet and found footage on YouTube of them entering the press conference, and I saw myself! I freeze-framed it and showed it to my partner, and she was in hysterics – I was in a jacket and tie as that's what you did back then, with long sideburns and a beard and reasonably long hair (I have none now!).

One of the shoots of mine that gets talked about more than others is Debbie Harry's Tea Party, at the Royal Garden in 1980. She was joined by the most famous female punk-rockers of the time – Chrissie Hynde of The Pretenders, Siouxsie Sioux of Siouxsie and the Banshees, Viv Albertine of The Slits, Pauline Black of the Selecter and Poly Styrene of X-Ray Spex.

I'd left London in 1976 to go and work in New York so I missed the punk thing altogether – it didn't really take off in the same way in New York. I'd seen Debbie Harry on stage once in New York, and this gorgeous, elfin girl in a tiny dress came on looking absolutely amazing. She cleared her throat and gobbed on the stage – and I didn't really understand that sort of punk thing…

But Debbie was lovely, and it was a great shoot. What was interesting was that the people arrived in reverse order to their fame – Debbie Harry arrived bang on the dot, then Chrissie Hynde, but it was Viv – who I've kept in touch with – who arrived about two-and-a-half hours late! It's a fun picture and someone is trying to put together a documentary on it and have me reshoot it, so I've been back at the Royal Garden to have a look around.

Frank Zappa was another one I shot at the Royal Garden. He was very, very odd. He was telling stories about dolphins with green rays coming out of their eyes and we were trying to keep a straight face. He was fascinating – he was obviously thinking on a different dimension and that's why his music is so weird and wonderful.

I also shot another band at the hotel who were very big at the time called Blood, Sweat and Tears (right). There are probably others too, but I would just scrawl the name of the artist and the date on the back of a negative in those days but rarely the location, so it's tough to remember sometimes!

HOLLYWOOD'S FINEST

—— **Dustin Hoffman arrived to find he had to field questions about his controversial movie.**

Dustin Hoffman was one of the hottest actors on the planet, having starred in *The Graduate* and *Midnight Cowboy*, when he was cast in the controversial 1971 film *Straw Dogs*.

Here he is at a press conference at the Royal Garden Hotel for the film, which was directed by Sam Peckinpah, and starred Hoffman as an American who moves to England to live with his wife in her birthplace in Cornwall, which causes resentment in the community.

Hoffman went on to further success in films such as *Kramer vs Kramer*, for which he won an Oscar for Best Actor, *Tootsie* and *Rain Man* – which won him a second Oscar.

PIRATES AHOY!
—— Kirk Douglas and Lesley-Anne Down managed a spot of publicity at the Royal Garden Hotel.

Kirk Douglas was one of the biggest stars going in the 1960s, having received three Best Actor Oscar nominations and starring in Stanley Kubrick's *Spartacus*.

In 1972 he arrived in London to promote his directorial debut, the pirate romp *Scalawag*. It starred Douglas himself and English actress Lesley-Anne Down in the lead roles, and they were at the Royal Garden Hotel for a photo shoot and press conference.

With love, [signature] Elton John

*THANK YOU FOR ALWAYS BEING MY FAMILY AND MY HOME AWAY FROM HOME.
Love Nigel Olsson [signature]*

*thank you as always
love to RGH !
[signature]*

*GOD BLESS RG,
A place we call home!!
[signature]*

*Thank you for always
providing us a safe
harbor in our stormy
Road life —
[signature]*

*YOU GUYS ARE A
HUGE PART OF
OUR LIFE.
THANKS TO ALL
AT R.G.H.,
[signature]
X
SPARTACUS NELSON*

GIVING ELTON SOME BACKING

—— One of the most famous backing bands are regular guests.

Elton John rightly receives all of the plaudits for being a stellar, six-decade-long rock 'n' roll megastar, but he also needs a little help from his friends.

This help comes in the form of his masterful backing band, who help to turn his live shows into the world-renowned extravaganzas they currently are. Life on the road with Elton means his band become accustomed to a certain standard, which is why they stay at the Royal Garden Hotel when playing in London.

During their last stay, the line-up included some of Elton's longest-serving band members, including guitarist Dave Johnstone, who has played over 2,000 concerts with Elton, and has worked with John Lennon, BB King and Eric Clapton. Also staying was drummer Nigel Olsson, one of Elton's original live 'power trio' in the 1970s. He left the band in the 1980s, swapping it for a life motor racing with Aston Martin and Ferrari, but the lure of music was too strong and he rejoined in 2000.

LOVE IS ALL AROUND

—— **At least it is when Wet Wet Wet come to stay at the hotel.**

Scottish band Wet Wet Wet have been regular guests at the Royal Garden Hotel since they formed in 1982.

Ever since their cover of The Troggs' *Love Is All Around* spent 15 weeks at the top of the British singles chart in 1994 they have remained one of Britain's most successful bands. They split up in 1999 but reformed five years later and have been touring ever since. Whenever they're in London they drop in to the hotel and have become familiar faces.

Hi this is marti from Wet Wet Wet I love staying with you the St H make this hotel happen for me from the smile I get from the front DOORMEN to the BARMAN Pure Class Love 2 Love Marti xxx

Great Days & Great times in this Hotel.... Thank-you....

My home from home. Best Wishes Tommy

GREAT PLACE PEOPLE IN RGH RULE, XTREMELY HELPFULL, GREAT ROOMS GREAT VIEWS LOVE WET.B X

LIVE AND LOUD
—— **The International Live Music Conference (ILMC) has been a big part of life at the hotel for over 15 years.**

The hotel's connection with music is further strengthened as, every spring since the turn of the century, it has played host to the ILMC, an annual conference dedicated to the global live music industry. With a huge range of events, panels, entertainment, networking, dinners and awards, the conference is the main meeting place for more than 1,000 professionals across the live music world to congregate, discuss their business and let their hair down in an environment where they feel right at home.

CALENDAR GIRLS
—— **Founding member of the Calendar Girls, Angela Knowles (left) on why the hotel has played an important part in her life.**

My first stay was when we came to London for the première of the film *Calendar Girls* at the Odeon Leicester Square in 2003. It was based on the story of when my husband John Baker passed away from non-Hodgkin's lymphoma, and me and my friends posed for a calendar to raise money for Leukaemia and Lymphoma Research (now renamed Bloodwise, and which the Royal Garden chose as their charity for one year). The night of the première was so exciting. I remember getting ready at the hotel beforehand and then all of the cars drawing up in front of the hotel and taking us to the Odeon. Everyone was so friendly and treated us like stars.

Each year at Christmas, the Leukaemia Research Fund holds a concert at the Royal Albert Hall called Carols with the Stars and all of the Calendar Girls are very fortunate to stay at the hotel as we all love it

there. We knew Kevin Costner was staying in the hotel at the same time as us once and it was a shame we didn't meet him as he is one of my favourite film stars. It is so friendly at the hotel. The first people you talk to on reception make you feel very special; they are so polite and cannot do enough for you. The rooms are excellent, the beds are so comfy and the bathrooms are fitted out with all the best fittings and everything is spotlessly clean. And the food is so tasty, especially the variety of food on offer at breakfast time.

My family have also stayed at the hotel and it is their favourite. Even my grandchildren love staying there and they base all of their opinions about other hotels against the Royal Garden benchmark. When they come to stay with me at my house I nearly achieve that benchmark but not quite!

ANOTHER GOLDEN ANNIVERSARY

—— **The Seekers came to stay during their Golden Jubilee Tour in 2014.**

The Aussie folk-pop group had a string of hits in the 1960s, including *Georgy Girl*, *Someday, One Day* and *I'll Never Find Another You* and were the first Australian group to have major chart success in the UK and the States. The 2014 tour took in dates across Australia and England, ending with two performances at the Royal Albert Hall.

ROOM AT THE HEARTBREAKERS HOTEL

—— Band booker Alan Newing gives thanks to the hotel.

I was rescued by the Royal Garden Hotel after a band booking went wrong.

It was 2002, ahead of the Concert for George at the Royal Albert Hall following the death of George Harrison. I called the hotel to arrange rooms for the artists performing at the event, which Eric Clapton was staging.

At the time I had no idea how many rooms, nor which type, I would need – and that's where the staff at the hotel rescued me. They suggested starting with X amount of doubles for sole use, Y amount of twins and Z amount of kings – and that we could, between us, just knock the rooms off the allocation as I received the requests (which were coming in direct from the performers, rather than through Clapton's office).

We had it pretty much down by the time people started arriving in the UK for rehearsals, when I received a call from the hotel one morning: "We've got Tom Petty and his band at reception… are they yours?"

I had been told that the band were making their own arrangements, but they had been told that I was arranging their accommodation! So I said "yes" and the staff managed to find them rooms! It's a story that, more than anything, illustrates how the Royal Garden has always been inventive and willing to work with an idea that takes shape over time. I don't think I have had that kind of rapport with any other hotel!

DO YA THINK I'M SEXY?

—— Rod Stewart, at the Royal Garden Hotel. In his pyjamas.

New Year's Day, 1974. Rod Stewart is one of the world's biggest rock stars, enjoying considerable success with the Faces and as a solo artist.

Known for his rasping voice, he shows off his playful side by posing in pyjamas at breakfast and twiddling with the TV controls in his room at the Royal Garden Hotel. The Faces were soon to head off on what would be their last tour together before splitting up, leaving him to concentrate on a solo career that has made him one of the biggest-selling musicians on the planet.

ROYAL WINDSOR

—— **English icon Barbara Windsor celebrated her 70th at the Royal Garden Hotel.**

Barbara Windsor has lived a life full of parties, so it was an honour for the Royal Garden to be chosen as the venue for her 70th birthday in 2007. Here she is seen arriving with her partner Scott Mitchell.

In a career that started in the 1950s on stage, she came to national fame with her appearances in nine *Carry On* films. In 1994 she was offered the role of a lifetime, as Queen Vic landlady Peggy Mitchell in *EastEnders* – a part she played for 16 years, becoming a national treasure in the process.

DANCING WITH THE STARS
—— The Bolshoi Ballet brought a touch of class to the Swinging Sixties.

The Royal Garden Hotel has not only welcomed rock 'n' roll stars and Hollywood legends in its illustrious history. In the 1960s it was the hotel of choice for a sophisticated Soviet invasion, as the world-famous Bolshoi Ballet toured London.

After a historic visit to London in 1956 – the first time a Soviet company had toured the West – the Bolshoi became regular visitors to Britain when Victor Hochhauser started organising their tours in 1963. They soon chose the Royal Garden as the perfect hotel to look after the large group of dancers and its sprawling entourage.

Staying with the Bolshoi at the Royal Garden Hotel in the 1960s was one of its all-time most famous prima ballerina, Nina Timofeyeva. Known for her athleticism and soaring jump, she had been part of that historic tour in '56 (she

got nine curtain calls after one performance at Covent Garden) and by the time the Royal Garden opened in 1965 she had become one of the great stars of ballet.

Timofeyeva, who died in 2014, graced the stage for more than 30 years, and embodied the spirit of the show must go on: in 1982 her husband Kirill Molchanov, General Director of the Bolshoi, died in his seat just before the start of a performance of *Macbeth* in which Timofeyeva was starring as Lady Macbeth. She was informed during the first interval, but insisted the performance continue.

The Bolshoi Ballet and Orchestra are returning to the Royal Opera House in July 2016, over 50 years since the Royal Garden Hotel opened its doors to one of the great dance companies of the 20th century.

Thank you. from. Mick Fleetwood

SIGN YOUR NAME...
—— **A host of musicians, actors, TV personalities and entertainers have left their mark on the hotel's history. And some of them have even left us a quite literal mark...**

Whether congratulating the hotel on its 50th, or simply saying thank you for a great stay, many of the hotel's high-profile guests have taken the time to pop their name in our guest book.

On these pages we have: musicians Jim Kerr, Billy Joel, Brian May, Engelbert Humperdinck, Mick Fleetwood, Chuck Berry, Kris Kristofferson, Motley Crüe, James Taylor, Tammy Wynette, Sacha Distel, Chris de Burgh, Robert Smith and Petula Clark; TV personalities Mike Yarwood, David Dimbleby, Les Dawson, Jimmy Tarbuck, Bruce Forsyth and Graham Norton; and stars of TV and film Felicity Kendal, Christopher Biggins, Sinead Cusack, Ben Kingsley, Hugh Bonneville, Jason Donovan, Joan Collins, Oliver Reed and Patrick Duffy. Can you work out who's who?

Billy Joel

HAPPY BIRTHDAY. ROYAL GARDEN. !!! 2015. Rock.!!!

David Dimbleby

Kris Kristofferson

thank you for all your care!! Sincerely

Best wishes Always — A Superstar INN EDDY!

Happy Anniversary!! My wonderful "Home from Home"....
Chris de B

To the Royal Garden! Thank you for a wonderful stay!

Love to the Royal Garden Hotel

Thank you for a wonderful breakfast—
Felicity Kendal.

all the best
and a bientôt
Sarah [...] 1979

Congratulations
to The
Royal Garden Hotel
from
Jim Kerr
Simple Minds

MÖTLEY CRÜE

HAPPY 50....
Sorry we
DESTROYED
so much stuff..
Nikki Sixx

We had a
wonderful time
Thanks!
Love ya!
Tammy Wynette

My very best wishes
to all at the Royal Garden.
Sincerely,
[signature] 1979

Thank you for a wonderful evening!
Best wishes
[signature]

Many a mile...
and a home abroad
chez the Royal
Garden. Always
[signature]

Best Wishes
Christopher Biggins
and mine
Sinéad Cusack

Best of luck
to the Royal Garden
[signature]

Best Wishes
[signature]

To all at the Royal Garden
thanks for feeding me so well
[signature]

To The Rojas +
fun & Room Service & chips
[signature]

x x x x x
one
Gin
each
STAR!!

Many thanks
I've stumbled the loos
here is truly wonderful
[signature]

HAPPY 50th!
THANKS FOR
LOOKIN
AFTER US!
[signature]
ROGER

We are going to the Crawl!
you've made our evening so
sweet
Lois
Sir Bill Kingdom
AO   Alexandra
AMA

My thanks
for the Gin and Tonic
hope to stay after
the "Farmers"
[signature]

Love
[signature]

SPORT

From being the official hotel of the 1966 World Cup to hosting the stars of rugby and cricket, via a spot of sumo, the Royal Garden Hotel has a remarkable sporting legacy

GOOD SPORTS

Bobby Moore clutches the Jules Rimet trophy and, with his England team-mates behind him, heads onto the main balcony at the Royal Garden Hotel. Below them thousands of ecstatic, wide-eyed football fans break into uproarious cheers, which turn into a roar when Moore lifts the cup above his head in celebration. The World Cup is England's.

Not long after Moore had been chaired by his team-mates on the Wembley pitch following England's 4-2 win over West Germany, the players had travelled on their coach through the streets of London, thronged with jubilant well-wishers, as the team made its way to where they and their families were to celebrate their success – the Royal Garden Hotel, the official hotel of the World Cup.

They had a reception at the hotel to celebrate their win, partied the night away in Soho and returned in the wee hours to the hotel and carried on celebrating until morning. Bleary-eyed, they then faced the press at the hotel to tell the story of the World Cup win which, 50 years on, remains the most iconic moment in English sporting history.

A year on from opening its doors, the Royal Garden was the chosen hotel for the most famous sportsmen in England. Not only did the players celebrate there, but England's press conferences were also held at the Royal Garden – which meant the attention of the world's media was concentrated on this new hotel at the heart of swinging London. From captain Moore to Bobby Charlton, until recently England's record goal-scorer, and from legendary goalkeeper Gordon Banks to the reserved, serious manager Alf Ramsey, the Royal Garden was the epicentre of the World Cup universe in July 1966.

The hotel was, of course, open to the public as England toasted their victory. So the stories don't just come from the mouths of the men who were on the Wembley pitch, but from guests who had booked in at the right time to catch a bit of history. As we shall see over the coming pages, some of them weren't even aware the England players were staying there…

The Royal Garden Hotel's part in England's finest sporting hour kicked off a long and illustrious association with sport. It has played host to FA Cup finalists throughout the years, as well as Premier League teams travelling to play nearby Chelsea. The hotel was also the base for the 1996 Euro Championships, when England agonisingly lost on penalties in the semi-finals to Germany, a Paul Gascoigne-slide away from their first major final since '66.

It's not all about football, though. In rugby union it is the home for New Zealand, Australia and South Africa when they play against England at Twickenham during the Autumn internationals. The same goes for cricket – the Royal Garden

often hosts visiting international teams when they're playing at Lord's or The Oval. It was also the base for Australia when they won the 1999 World Cup, and home to teams during the Champions Trophy in 2004 and 2013.

In interviews over the next few pages with some of the cricket and rugby stars who have stayed at the hotel, they all share one thing in common when it comes to the Royal Garden: a true affection for the hotel, which has led to the teams coming back each time they're in London. Sports teams appreciate familiarity, so when they've settled on somewhere they like they'll keep on returning. Many call it a home from home, with several coming back to the hotel even after they've retired from international sport.

While the Royal Garden's association with the world's leading team sports has seen some legendary sporting figures pass through the hotel's corridors, it's not just football, cricket and rugby that have connections with the hotel. The sporting history of the hotel is rather more diverse than that.

One of the fondest stories is from the time the Royal Garden welcomed the first-ever sumo wrestling tournament to be held outside of Japan, in 1991. The hotel housed all of the wrestlers and plenty of media and officials, with certain weight adjustments having to be made in the rooms in order to make their stay a comfortable one. There are also stories from the worlds of tennis and rowing, including a terrifying Atlantic crossing.

While sport may not be everyone's cup of tea, the history of the Royal Garden Hotel is full of stories that transcend the games and reveal fun anecdotes and tales of derring-do.

Plus, well, it's been 50 years of hurt since England won the football World Cup, so there's absolutely nothing wrong with taking a look back at 1966 and celebrating the Royal Garden Hotel's unique involvement in sporting history.

Facing page, top to bottom: Royal Garden Pastry Chef Signor Chianese creates a World Cup-themed cake in 1966; football manager Lawrie McMenemy and jockey Bob Champion with 1981 Grand National winner Aldaniti. This page: tennis stars including Chris Evert, Billie Jean King and Tracy Austin gather in front of the hotel; former Australian cricket captains Ricky Ponting and Steve Waugh; the 2014 Australian rugby union squad.

LONDON GROUP 1		MIDLANDS GROUP 2		NORTH WEST GROUP 3		NORTH EAST GROUP 4	
JULY		JULY		JULY		JULY	
11th ENGLAND	v URUGUAY	12th W.GERMANY	v SWITZERLAND	12th BULGARIA	v BRAZIL	12th U.S.S.R.	v N.KOREA
13th FRANCE	v MEXICO	13th SPAIN	v ARGENTINA	13th HUNGARY	v PORTUGAL	13th CHILE	v ITALY
15th URUGUAY	v FRANCE	15th SWITZERLAND	v SPAIN	15th BRAZIL	v HUNGARY	15th N.KOREA	v CHILE
16th MEXICO	v ENGLAND	16th ARGENTINA	v W.GERMANY	16th PORTUGAL	v BULGARIA	16th ITALY	v U.S.S.R.
19th MEXICO	v URUGUAY	19th ARGENTINA	v SWITZERLAND	19th PORTUGAL	v BRAZIL	19th ITALY	v N.KOREA
20th FRANCE	v ENGLAND	20th SPAIN	v W.GERMANY	20th HUNGARY	v BULGARIA	20th CHILE	v U.S.S.R.

66

WORLD CUP DRAW

QUICK ON THE DRAW

—— It was not just during the World Cup proper in July when the hotel was the centre of the world's attention. Earlier in the year, in January, the footballing world came together to see who would be playing against whom later in the year.

BROTHERS IN ARMS

Several of England's World Cup stars have recalled the celebrations at the Royal Garden Hotel in autobiographies and interviews over the years. Alan Ball said in *Playing Extra Time*: "The biggest night for celebration came after the Jules Rimet Trophy was in England's custody. To ride on the coach to the Royal Garden Hotel, where the official function was taking place, was an experience never to be forgotten.

"I was truly staggered by the people lining the pavements all the way, cheering and waving their balloons and flags. It rammed home to me just what this win meant to the country. Tens of thousands of people brought the traffic to a standstill."

And Bobby Charlton, in *My England Years*, remembered: "It was wonderful to be reunited with Norma [his wife] at the Royal Garden Hotel on Kensington High Street, where we had been moved for the post-game celebrations, and to see the pride of my mother Cissie and father Robert, and to catch everyone's excitement when we walked out onto the balcony to show off the Jules Rimet trophy and wave to the crowd.

"It was then maybe I saw the first clear indication that Alf Ramsey had finally relaxed in the knowledge that he had achieved all that he had set out to do. As the waves of cheers crashed in, he began to smile in a way that resembled a young, gratified boy more than an old pro who had realised how many things could go wrong. And even as all this was happening, inevitably I suppose, so many flashpoints of the game and its aftermath kept coming back to me. I remember thinking that each one had to be stored away and kept forever.

"One of them was Jack [Charlton] and me on the lap of honour, feeling suddenly so knackered, and my brother putting his arm around my shoulders and saying: 'Well, what about that, kiddo?'. 'Our lives will never be the same again, I don't suppose,' I replied."

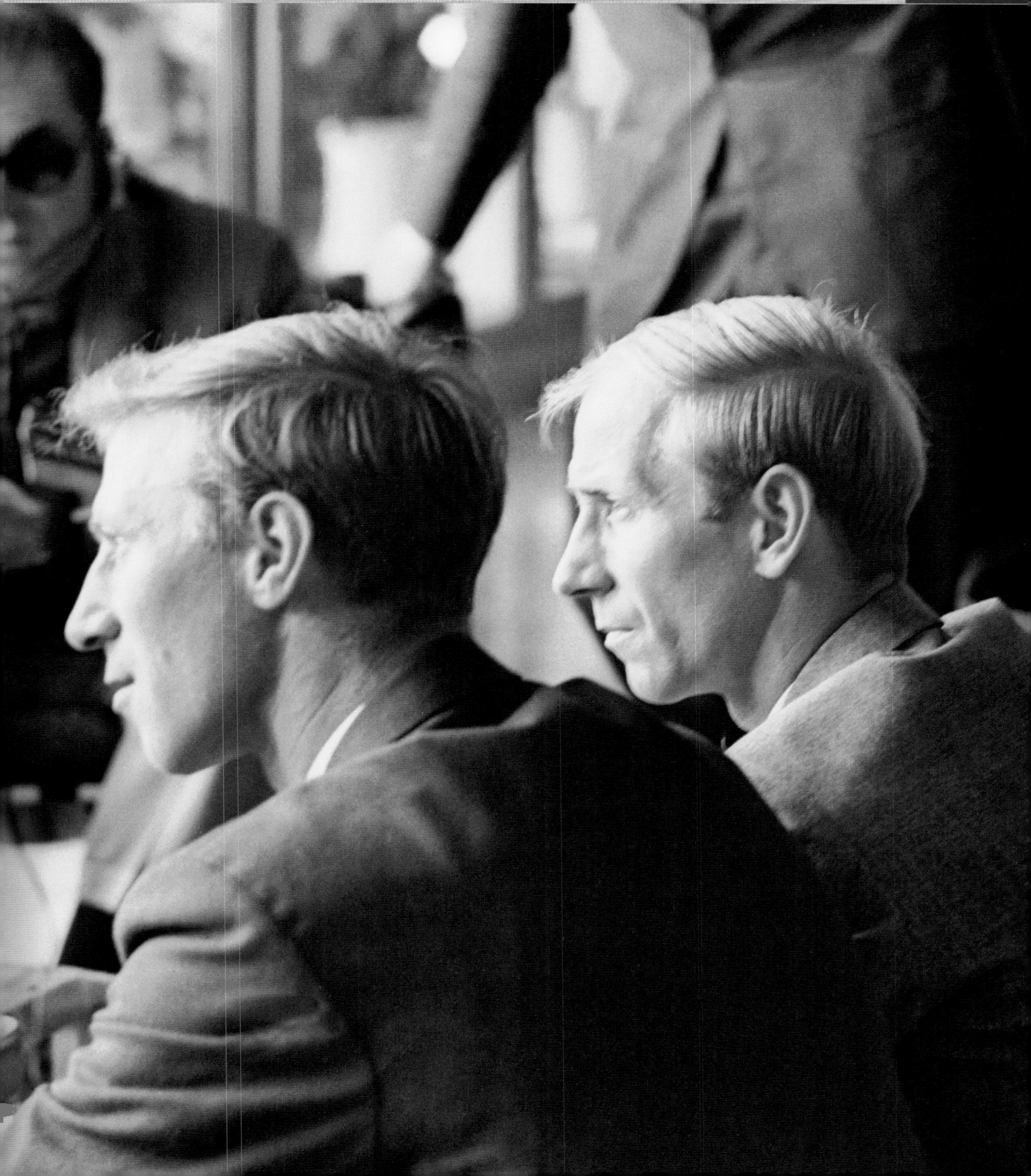

ONCE IN A LIFETIME

—— The reception at the hotel was a joyous occasion. The team and their families, Alf Ramsey and his wife, politicians, friends, reporters, everyone had the time of their lives....

OH WHAT A NIGHT!

—— Regular Royal Garden guest Cathy Matos ended up celebrating with the England team by a rather circuitous route.

I married a Puerto Rican pilot on the day of the World Cup final.

I was 20, and I knew nothing about football. When I talked to any men about the wedding date they'd stand there totally incredulous. It's World Cup final day! You're out of your mind! Nobody can get married on World Cup final day!

So we had the wedding, and it poured with rain of course – and those who wanted to watch the game managed to watch it at the reception. But it was after the wedding that the fun really started. We had planned to go to a lovely olde-worlde hotel in Crawley that night, but when we got there they put us in an annexe, so it wasn't olde-worlde at all!

So I moaned and groaned. And my husband Joe – who I'm no longer married to – said to me in the morning: "Well that's it, we're no longer staying here, we're going to get in the car and find somewhere else." And off we went to London, without a clue where we were going. We come off the Hammersmith flyover, and we're coming down into Kensington and we see the Royal Garden Hotel and Joe says: "Right, we're staying here". I say: "We can't stay here!". It looked huge and very expensive. So a screech of brakes, and Joe says: "No, we're staying here."

He checked in and we were standing in the lift and he was saying: "Jesus Christ it's £10 a night!" It was a fortune in those days! But I was blown away by it all, it was absolutely wonderful – although he kept chuntering about the price!

I walked down in the morning and there were hundreds of photographers! I didn't realise all of the England players were staying at the hotel, and I was completely oblivious to all of this – I didn't know what it meant to win the World Cup. But it turned into a really fantastic, fun day because they involved me in all of the events and stuff that they were getting up to. They were all drunk and running around, but all very well behaved! It went on all day and I had a great time, but Joe felt very left out because he wasn't a football fan, and he didn't understand what it meant. I'd never known such an atmosphere in England.

It was such a comedown the next morning though, as I just had to meet my mother at Tesco on the corner. Talk about coming down from such a height!

SHOCK TACTICS

—— **Lawrie McMenemy, Southampton's manager in the 1976 FA Cup Final against Manchester United, remembers the Royal Garden's part in one of the greatest Cup shocks in English football. The hotel was, and still is, a regular venue for the country's top football clubs when they play in London.**

We went into the final as real underdogs. We were in the old second division – we'd been relegated the season before – and United under Tommy Docherty were a good young side who had done really well in the league. We'd been completely written off by most people.

We were staying at the Royal Garden, and it was a very sunny day. The atmosphere was very relaxed, and that helped the players. My wife, Anne, hadn't been so relaxed when she arrived at the hotel as she was terrified having to drive down into the car park! Although she did later meet Donny Osmond, and he sent a signed photo up to our room, which I think made up for it!

Our goalkeeper, Ian Turner, had a wonderful game and was saving everything, using his head, his knee – anything to stop a goal! And then Bobby Stokes, who had been missing chances galore since the semi-final – it had almost become a standing joke he'd missed so

many – went clean through in the 83rd minute and won it for us. They called it one of the greatest FA Cup shocks, and it was the first trophy in Southampton's history, so you can imagine the celebrations were pretty special!

I took the team to a nightclub to celebrate, and then back to the hotel. It was a great evening, and I remember coming back downstairs from the directors' private party and I got a call from Tommy Docherty, who wanted to congratulate me. That was really fabulous of him, and I told him so. He said: "Don't get me wrong, I'm crying". I also told him I hoped United would win the Cup the following season, which they did – and they knocked us out on their way!

I've stayed in the Royal Garden regularly since then, and I love the atmosphere there. The staff are all so friendly, they'd do anything for you. It's a special place, and holds really brilliant memories for me.

MAGNIFICENT SEVEN

—— **Former Australia captain Nathan Sharpe has been a regular visitor since first stopping by in 2005.**

The Royal Garden is an amazing hotel, rich with history and tradition. I remember when I first stayed there in 2005 it gave me a real sense that this was exactly what a top-class London hotel should be like.

I stayed there seven times, as we would always make a point of being there for every Spring tour we made. We had other options, but from the first time we stayed there it was clear we'd keep on returning. It's important for a team to find a hotel they like and then return as familiarity is crucial. Every single player looks forward to staying there because they know everything will be of the highest quality. The staff are fantastic, the rooms are so comfortable, the location is perfect and nothing is too much for the hotel to help you with.

The final time I played at Twickenham, in 2012, was one of my last-ever games for Australia and I was captain at the time. We were staying at the Royal Garden and it was an intense, emotional week. It was my last crusade against the old foe. We were lucky enough to get the win 20-14 in a really good match so I have very fond memories of that game and the week surrounding it at the Royal Garden.

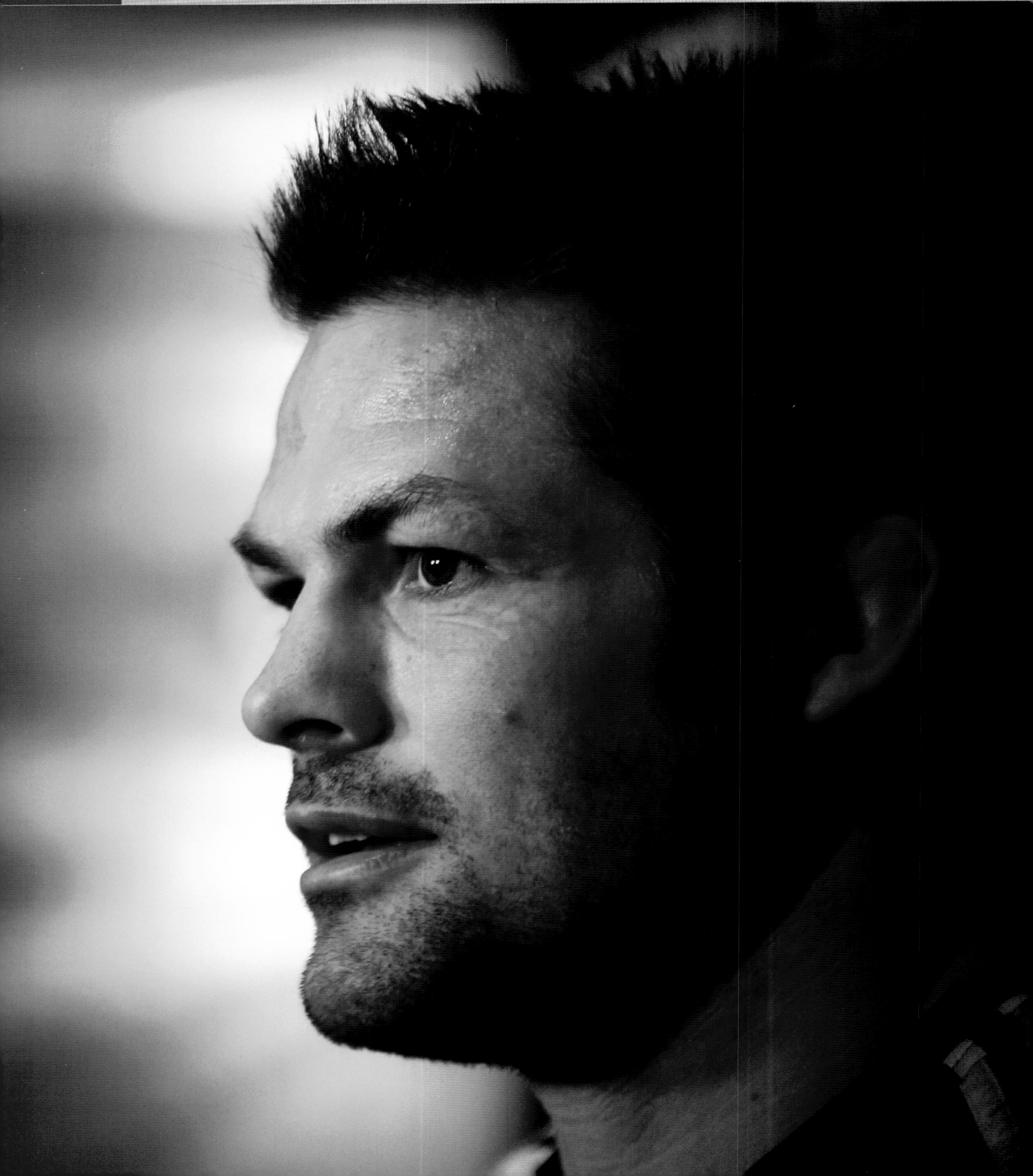

GREAT EXPECTATIONS

—— **Rugby legend and the sport's most capped player, Richie McCaw, who recently led New Zealand to their second successive World Cup victory, is a big fan of the hotel.**

I first stayed at the Royal Garden hotel in 2005 on our Grand Slam tour, when we managed to become the first side to win the Grand Slam – beating all four sides – in the professional era. We beat Wales, Ireland, England and Scotland on that tour, although England was the toughest and closest match (I missed it because of a head injury).

My first impression of the hotel was that it's in a great location, right on the park, which is a great setting and nice and close to all the sights. The rooms we stay in are great and we have always been welcomed when we come and stay.

We usually get one day off a week during a Test build-up, so it is a chance to get out and see the sights. Over the years I have always had friends living in London doing their Overseas Experience, so I often used that time to catch up with them. Over the years I have been coming to London I have got around most of the sights. I have stayed on at the end of tours for a holiday and to catch up with friends and on three or four occasions have stayed at the Royal Garden as it is handy for everywhere.

Because we've stayed at the hotel a lot, it's great to know what to expect and that we have all the right areas for the team meetings etc. Having been to London a number of times it is nice going somewhere familiar. We spend some of our down time playing cards either in each other's rooms at the hotel or we find a café and play to kill time. I've always enjoyed touring the UK and especially our weeks in London. Having had some success in games helps and it has always coincided with staying at the hotel – on a few occasions we have had our last game in England for the year so have had some celebrations and end-of-season parties at the hotel bars, which is always fun.

I've been lucky enough to play in six wins over England at Twickenham during my career, and I'd say the victory in 2013, when we won 30-22, is one of the most satisfying as we had been beaten the previous year. To turn that around at the end of what ended up being an unbeaten year was great.

This shot of Richie was taken during a press conference at the Royal Garden.

SNOW BUSINESS

Hundreds of miles from sunny Cape Town, the South African rugby team bravely get in their full kit – shorts and all – to pose in Kensington Gardens on a snowy November day in 2010.

The cold weather didn't put the team off their rugby, though. A few days earlier they beat England 21-11 at Twickenham, with fly-half Morné Steyn scoring 11 points without the need for gloves or a woolly hat.

UP THE GARDEN PATH

New Zealand have dominated international rugby union for the last couple of decades, and fly-half Aaron Cruden is another in a long line of super-talented young players to emerge.

He poses here in Kensington Gardens after a media session at the Royal Garden Hotel. Two days later he scored a try and kicked two penalties as the All Blacks beat England 24-21 in a thrilling encounter at Twickenham.

FAMILIAR FACES

—— The Royal Garden Hotel has been a home from home for Australia's cricketers ever since they won the World Cup in 1999. The team stayed there then and does so still whenever they are touring and in town, and strong relationships have developed between the hotel and Cricket Australia. Despite England coming out on top in Ashes contests since 2005, London has been a happy hunting ground for the Aussies and brings back fond memories for former captains Ricky Ponting and Steve Waugh, as well as former Australian team manager Steve Bernard.

Royal Garden Hotel. Happy 50th.

I first stayed here with the team for the 1999 World Cup. The week leading up to the final was huge, and that was obviously a great time to stay at the hotel so we've got really good memories of that. The after-party at the hotel after we'd won was something else. We were at the top of the hotel and it was just a really great night.

From then the Australian team has always stayed here for every tour, which says a lot about the hotel. For us it feels like our London home really. After the Lord's or Oval Tests you'd always have a beer in the bar as a team, and we have fond memories of that – especially as we always seem to do so well at Lord's. If you've got good

memories of a place then you like returning. It's the same as at a certain cricket ground – if you've got good memories of it then it makes you feel more comfortable when you next go back, and I think the association with the 1999 World Cup immediately means there are so many fine memories of coming back to London and staying at the Royal Garden. The people's faces at the hotel are familiar, and there are certain people you remember and they're all so helpful and friendly. It's great for our families too. With the park next door it's perfect for wives and kids to do stuff too while we're playing, and my daughter's first overseas trip was to London and she stayed at the Royal Garden with us.

BASE CAMP

—— Former Australian captain Steve Waugh is one of cricket's all-time legends.

The Royal Garden Hotel is basically our home away from home on a long tour.

You like to know where you're staying, because you get the feel of the restaurants around the place and the hotel staff, who are amazing. You want a place where you know you can come and relax, you can chill out and you can go for a walk and you feel you're nice and settled in your environment.

A lot of the squad in 1999, when we were here for the World Cup, had families and the park is great when you have kids. It makes it feel like you're not really in a hotel. I think the number one thing about this hotel is the location because you've got the park just 15 metres from the front door. I remember the team going for a number of walks before games, that's where we would talk.

The party we had at the hotel after we won the World Cup in 1999 was legendary, but it was bittersweet for me. It went on into the early hours of the morning, and one minute I was carrying the World Cup around and the next I was taking a phonecall at 2.30 in the morning to tell me my grandfather had passed away. It was a night of incredible contrasting emotions.

There's a reason why the Australian team still set up their base at the Royal Garden, and I think it's a really great relationship that's provided some great memories of our stays in London.

These shots of Ricky and Steve were taken at the Royal Garden Hotel in the summer of 2015.

EXCEPTIONAL
—— **Steve Bernard was Australia's Team Manager from 1998 to 2001.**

We first stayed at the Royal Garden Hotel during the 1999 World Cup [the photo above is of captain Steve Waugh with the trophy], and again in 2001 during the Ashes tour that year. During our various stays at the Royal Garden, the players found it to be a fantastic place to stay, and saw it as their little home away from home. The position by the Royal Gardens was wonderful, Kensington High Street was an exciting area, and the staff at the hotel were friendly, accommodating and always ready to assist with the various issues I would experience as the Team Manager.

In 2002, the England and Wales Cricket Board decided they would sign a deal with a hotel chain, who all future visiting teams would be obligated to stay with. When I informed the various Australian team members of this

change, there was genuine upset that we would have to move from our beloved London headquarters. They asked me if Cricket Australia could make representation to the ECB for special dispensation for the Australian team to continue to stay at the Royal Garden. Fortunately for the team, the ECB agreed that because of our close relationship with the hotel they would make an exception for us, and the team could continue to stay at the Royal Garden.

I am happy to say that the Australian team once again stayed at the hotel during this year's Ashes. I have moved on after 13 years as Team Manager and after many enjoyable stays at the Royal Garden. However, when I return to London for a visit, I continue to stay there – it is one of the great hotels of the world.

FACING THE PRESS

—— **It is not just Australia's cricketers who have found the Royal Garden to their liking. Indeed most international teams have stayed there at one time or another over the past 15 years and when England has hosted a world tournament, such as the ICC Champions Trophy in 2004 and 2013, the hotel has seen a vast array of nationalities making it their camp.**

AB de Villiers, one of the finest batsmen in the world, leads a press conference at the Royal Garden ahead of the ICC Champions Trophy 2013. The South African team has often stayed at the hotel when touring England – and they have happy memories in the UK, as they haven't lost a Test series here since 1998. However, de Villiers and South Africa didn't have luck on their side at the Champions Trophy. After stumbling through to the semi-finals following a tied match against West Indies, they came

DRESSED TO IMPRESS

Here, tennis designer extraordinaire Ted Tilling poses with tennis stars (left to right) Virginia Wade, Evonne Goolagong, Rosemary Casals and Billie Jean King at the Royal Garden Hotel in June 1973 ahead of Wimbledon.

British-born Tilling, who played at Wimbledon, turned his hand to designing women's tennis clothing and 12 female Wimbledon champions wore his dresses between 1959 and 1979 – including King, who would go on to win the singles title in '73. He also designed American tennis player Chris Evert's dress for her 1979 wedding to British player John Lloyd.

His designs were banned from Wimbledon on several occasions as they were thought too risqué by the authorities, but he was inducted into the Tennis Hall Of Fame in 1986.

RATHER THEM THAN US

John Ridgway and Chay Blyth, both members of the British army, attend a luncheon in their honour at the Royal Garden Hotel, in October 1966. Their achievement? Becoming the first duo to row across the Atlantic.

After initially being rejected by journalist David Johnstone to be part of his attempt to row the Atlantic, Ridgway decided to take on the challenge himself, and Blyth took the plunge to go along with him. They'd already won a 24-hour canoe race down the Thames, but Blyth's only experience at sea had been crossing the English Channel by steamer.

They left Cape Cod on 4 June 1966 in their 20ft open dory 'English Rose III', with a crowd of thousands giving them a splendid send-off. Johnstone had left some two weeks earlier attempting the same feat, with crew member John Hoare.

Ridgway and Blyth battled huge storms – including Hurricane Alma, the first spring hurricane in 60 years – enormous waves and whales, as well as fatigue and hunger. Incredibly, they learned the result of the football World Cup from the captain of a passing Shell tanker.

Finally, after 3,000 miles and 92 days at sea, they reached the Irish coast in dreadful conditions. News of their adventure spread quickly, and further publicity was created when Johnstone's and Hoare's boat was found upside down in the Atlantic – the two men were never found. The last entry in their logbook was on the day Ridgway and Blyth made land, and it recorded the approach of a gale, fast becoming a hurricane.

Ridgway twice went on to circumnavigate the globe, while Blyth became the first person to sail westwards around the world non-stop in 1971.

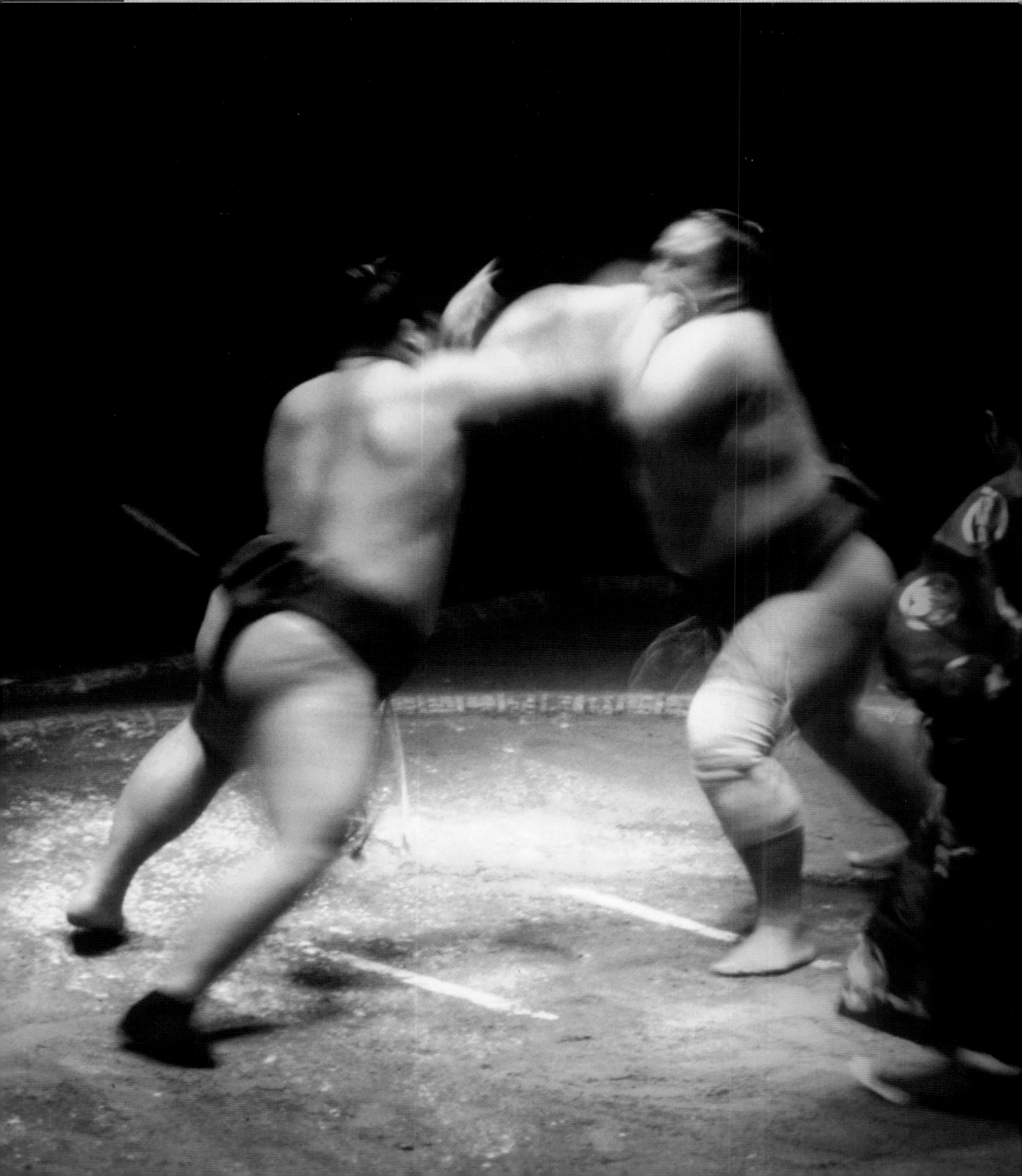

INVASION OF THE GIANTS

—— Belinda Boyd, who handled the sumo PR, remembers when the big men came to town.

I handled PR for the Royal Garden Hotel in the early 1990s, and one unique event that really stands out was the first-ever sumo tournament (honbasho) outside Japan in the sport's 1500-year history. Held at the Royal Albert Hall as part of London's first Japan Festival in October 1991, the contestants (or rikishi) were from Makunouchi, Japan's elite sumo division.

The tournament lasted five days and was sold out. The Royal Garden Hotel hosted the top 40 rikishi, their entourage and the international press, and for a while the hotel became known as the 'Royal Garden rikishi stable'. The event attracted an enormous amount of media attention here and around the globe as this was a world first. Crowds would gather outside to catch a glimpse of the hotel's unfamiliar guests as they went sightseeing in High Street Kensington wearing their traditional cotton robes (yukata) and wooden sandals (geta), which made a distinctive clip-clop sound.

The hotel management started planning their stay months before to ensure the wrestlers were not only comfortable but could also continue to follow their very strict way of life. Japanese receptionists were employed, beds were increased to nine feet and strengthened, lifts, lavatories and chairs were weight-tested, while larger detachable shower heads were fitted in the bathrooms as the usual ones wouldn't cover the wrestlers' bodies. The hotel even sourced special giant bars of soap measuring 6" x 4" which were attached to ropes and they commissioned extra-large porcelain soap dishes.

All of this generated immense coverage for the hotel: journalists were fascinated by the sumo wrestlers' size, diet and their regimented way of life. The Palace Suite was transformed into their 'restaurant'. The hotel's brigade had been instructed to produce two high-calorific meals a day (breakfast and supper), using a mix of both Japanese and English ingredients. This went down well with Konishiki Yasokichi, the heaviest-ever wrestler at that time – weighing in at 37.5 stone – who said: "Usually in Japan we don't have breakfast. Foreign food has been good but we get one meal too much I guess". Before breakfast they would fix their hair in top-knots and after each meal they would have a siesta to help them increase their weight.

Several press conferences were held at the hotel and two of the most popular wrestlers were the Hawaiians Konishiki, who had earned his nickname 'The Dump Truck', and Akebono Taro, who went on to become the first non-Japanese-born wrestler to reach yokozuna, the highest rank in sumo.

It was a privilege to have worked so closely with the Royal Garden Hotel, the sumos and their support team. Despite so many demands on their time they were always courteous and handled requests with patience, professionalism and good humour.

NAME IN THE BOOK

—— Sportsmen are used to signing autographs so have been only too happy to oblige when we've asked them to say a word or two.

See if you can decipher the scrawls of the Manchester United squad of 1981-82, England's leading wicket-taker Jimmy Anderson, West Indian greats Clyde Walcott and Clive Lloyd, legendary English middle distance runners Dave Moorcroft, Sebastian Coe and Roger Bannister, or Liverpool and England's Steven Gerrard.

Dave Moorcroft

To All at the Royal
Garden Hotel,
Thank you for always
making my stay relaxed
+ comfortable !!
Happy 50th !!
Best Wishes

HAPPY 50th BIRTHDAY
TO THE ROYAL GARDENS

Best Wishes

8

With every best wish
Sebastian Coe

And from me too
Roger Bannister

Thanks for a wonderful
Day.
Best wishes

PEOPLE IN HIGH PLACES

As befits its name and the history of Kensington, the Royal Garden Hotel has been no stranger to royal visitors and politicians over the first 50 years of its existence

Well before there was a hotel on the site, royalty was rarely far away. Monarchs William and Mary moved into Kensington Palace (then Nottingham House, built in the early 1600s) in 1689 and William hired Christopher Wren to turn it into a royal residence. The architect added pavilions to each corner of the existing house and built a new westward extending courtyard.

Under George I, the house was renovated as he felt it to be too old-fashioned and this work was continued by his son, George II. However, following the death of Queen Caroline, the Palace was abandoned by the country's royalty, although Victoria was born there and lived there until she became Queen.

In more recent times, the Palace has been home to the Prince and Princess of Wales, Charles and Diana, Princess Margaret, the Duke and Duchess of Gloucester and Kent, and of course the Duke and Duchess of Cambridge, William and Kate.

The hotel has also seen the arrival of a succession of Middle Eastern princes, many of whom have considered it almost as their second home. Former General Manager James Brown says: "The younger brother of the current ruler of Dubai, Sheikh Ahmed, became resident in the hotel for months. He and his entourage would come in and take a whole wing. After three or four years of this, we got to learn that the Sheikh had bought a house somewhere in the High Street and it was being done up. He stayed there exactly five days and then checked back in here, saying: 'Forget the house. This is far better for me'."

The hotel's location, neighbouring Kensington Place and in close proximity to many leading embassies, has made it a magnet for visiting dignitaries. Most recently, there have been visits from representatives of the Elders, an independent group of global leaders, formed in 2007 by Nelson Mandela and chaired by Kofi Annan, who work for peace and human rights, and bring with them a wealth of diverse expertise and experience.

Many guests come to the hotel for the privacy it affords but there have still been a large number of high-profile visits over the years. Lord Louis Mountbatten; the Queen Mother taking afternoon tea; the King of Norway; the Queen of Denmark; Vladimir Putin; King Juan Carlos of Spain; Kenneth Kaunda and Robert Mugabe arguing over who had the better accommodation: the list is a genuine who's who, but here are just a few examples.

Facing page: General Manager Jonathan Lowrey with former US President Jimmy Carter, a representative of The Elders. This page: Prime Minister Harold Wilson addresses the FIFA Congress; the PM with his trademark pipe; Princess Anne plants a tree in Kensington Gardens.

Princess at planting ceremony

THE Royal Garden lived up to its regally horticultural name recently when Princess Margaret, pictured right, took part in a tree planting ceremony in Kensington Gardens.

The event had been organised by General Manager James Brown and was the culmination of five months planning, the final aim of which was to replenish stocks lost after last year's devastating hurricane.

Eight children from around the world helped in the ceremony by planting trees native to their homelands. They were all sons and daughters of diplomats living in London and came from Canada, Finland, France, Italy, the Netherlands, Norway, Sweden and the USA.

THAT WORLD CUP VICTORY (AGAIN!)

There's nothing new under the sun. Politicians making sure they are associated with sporting success may seem like something from our spin-doctor age but back in 1966, as England beat the World, not realising they would not do so again for at least 50 years, Prime Minister Harold Wilson and Minister of Sport Denis Howell made sure they were there or thereabouts, pressing the flesh and smiling for the cameras. Wilson was no stranger to the Royal Garden, also addressing the FIFA Congress in the Palace Suite.

THE LINK MAN

John Sweeney, a long-serving linkman at the Royal Garden in the early '80s, was slightly startled when Princess Michael of Kent, a regular visitor to the Steiner hairdressing salon in the hotel, stopped to chat to him as she left the hotel to return home. He was even more surprised when she called the hotel to thank John for keeping her driveway spick and span after she had seen him cleaning up as she drove from Kensington Palace!

John was also befriended by King Hussein of Jordan, who heard that John had been looking for a particular book on his country. The King very kindly sent it round to the hotel with personal greetings inked on the fly cover…

A FAIR AND PEACEFUL WORLD

Former Secretary General of the United Nations Kofi Annan has been a regular visitor to the hotel in recent times, as part of his work with the Kofi Annan Foundation.

The Foundation, founded in 2007, mobilises political will to overcome threats to peace, development and human rights.

From his time working at the United Nations, Annan knew that many of these major issues are closely linked: "There can be no long-term development without peace and no long-term peace without development. And neither are sustainable without the rule of law."

By bringing together people from different sectors, the Foundation aims to overcome the sometimes seemingly insurmountable problems faced by millions of individuals across the world.

OFF TO SEE THE QUEEN

Crown Prince Vong Savang of Laos accompanied by his wife Princess Manilay, stayed at the Royal Garden Hotel in 1970 and he is pictured here heading off to dine with the Queen at Buckingham Palace.

A DAY TO REMEMBER

The Royal Garden Hotel was treated to a very special visit from the Duke and Duchess of Cambridge in October 2014. The Royal couple came to welcome The President of the Republic of Singapore and Mrs Tony Tan Keng Yam on behalf of The Queen. President Tony Tan Keng Yam is the first Singaporean President to make an official visit to the United Kingdom as the guest of Her Majesty The Queen.

General Manager Jonathan Lowrey says: "We were honoured that the President and Mrs Tan chose to stay with us. The Duke and Duchess were welcomed to the hotel by our owners and visited the President and Mrs Tan in their suite. The visit went smoothly and the Duchess was even heard to comment that she had always wondered what it was like in the hotel, having passed it so frequently on her way to and from home!"

PRESIDENT
REPUBLIC OF SINGAPORE

1 August 2015

To the team at Royal Garden Hotel, London

My wife and I send our warmest wishes on the occasion of the hotel's 50th anniversary.

Thank you for your impeccable service and warm hospitality to our family and the Singaporean community in London. We look forward to many more memorable stays and meals at the Royal Garden Hotel in the years and decades to come.

DIGNITARIES FROM SINGAPORE

Many Singaporean dignitaries have passed through the revolving doors of the hotel, such as the Minister Mentor of Singapore, the late Mr Lee Kuan Yew (above), and the current Prime Minister Lee Hsien Loong (left).

Executive Director Jennifer Carmichael recalls: "It was such an honour to meet Minister Mentor Lee Kuan Yew. He was a very engaging person and showed a genuine interest in people. He would take time to converse with staff members, often asking questions about their jobs and, if they were from abroad, what it was that had brought them to London."

The Royal Garden's Company Representative Joan Lau adds: "We work closely with the Singapore High Commission but have also been delighted to welcome dignitaries from all over the world. As a Singaporean, I can't deny it was especially exciting to have had Mr Lee Kuan Yew and Prime Minister Lee Hsien Loong staying here. Senior members of the Government of Singapore stay with us on official visits and also in their private capacity."

REGULAR ROYALS

The Duke of Edinburgh and Princesses Anne are regular visitors to the Royal Garden, as was Princess Margaret, in their capacities as guests of honour or patrons of various charities. A young princess Anne is seen arriving at the hotel in 1972, while Princess Margaret planted a tree in Kensington Gardens after the great hurricane of 2008. Meanwhile, General Manager James Brown welcomes Prince Philip to the hotel in 1978.

OUR GUESTS

We talk to the people who really matter, the guests, about their tales of romance, reunions and regular visits to their favourite hotel

THE TRUE STARS

No matter how many glamorous celebrities step through the entrance, no matter how many sporting events it hosts, no matter how many politicians and royals make big decisions in its conference rooms, a hotel is nothing without its guests.

Without them, a hotel would have no life, no character, no story to tell. Which is why the Royal Garden Hotel treats all of its guests like royalty. On average the Royal Garden welcomes 3,500 staying guests a week in its 394 rooms. There's a whole lot of tales from inside the walls of those bedrooms; and even more so when you move out of the bedrooms and into the restaurants. With 50 years of history there are enough stories to fill several novels, and we've tried to fit in as many as we could over the next few pages to give a feel for what it is that keeps so many guests returning to the Royal Garden Hotel.

From newlyweds honeymooning there, to a carefully planned engagement that was almost scuppered by an unfortunate injury to the fiancée's wedding finger, to a couple who met while the future groom was working on the construction of the hotel back in 1964, the last 50 years have brought plenty of moving and amusing stories of romance.

Stories of spending Christmases at the Royal Garden, of three generations meeting up in the restaurant and of a young child enchanted by the view from a room over Kensington Gardens shows the role the hotel plays in bringing families together for special occasions.

An owner of a small business collecting an award at a ceremony at the hotel, a lady falling in love with the music of John Wilson – and with her husband-to-be: both tales of the element of wonder and hope that can arise from a memorable trip to a memorable hotel.

And, if a hotel is nothing without its guests, it is also nothing without its staff. Over the coming pages it is clear that the hotel staff are loved by guests just as much as the guests are loved by the hotel.

So whether this is your first, second or even your tenth trip to the Royal Garden Hotel, perhaps one of your stories will be appearing in the 100th anniversary book…

THE GIRL IN THE KIOSK

—— **Howard Tait on first setting eyes on his future wife.**

The Royal Garden Hotel didn't just play a small part in my life, it set the course of my future, and in the most wonderful way. It was back in the early 1970s when I was a plucky young man, fresh out of university, and eager to make my mark in the cut and thrust world of advertising.

Money was tight and I lived in a modest flat near Streatham Ice Rink. Hungry to succeed, I would often wander down to the Royal Garden Hotel after work and soak up the atmosphere of a life I longed to be part of. Standing back, in my ill-fitting suit, I would envy the wealth of celebrities checking in and out. Sean Connery with a beautiful Bond girl on his arm; Robert De Niro heading up to the lavish rooftop restaurant; Olivia de Havilland drifting fragrantly by to relax in her luxury suite; Malcolm McDowell after the amazing launch of *A Clockwork Orange*.

The Royal Garden Hotel had it all, and if I couldn't afford a room I'd have the next best thing – an *Evening Standard* from the nice little bookshop/kiosk in the foyer (long since gone).

It was there that I first laid eyes on her. The gorgeous blonde with the captivating smile standing behind the counter. Of course, I would have to up my game. This was a lady used to dealing with the very rich; the successful, beautiful people. So I ditched my paper and asked for a *Horse & Hound* instead.

It took me weeks, and countless copies of *Country Life*, to pluck up the courage to ask her out, but luck was on my side and the beautiful Kathy Sanderson – sales assistant at the Royal Garden News Kiosk – eventually agreed to a date.

The rest, as they say, is history. We went out, we fell in love, and when my career took off I did what I'd always promised I'd do. I booked a romantic meal for two at the Royal Garden's rooftop restaurant – a really amazing experience, especially in those days.

Kathy and I have been married now for 38 years. We have a wonderful life, a beautiful daughter Natalie, and we've continued to visit our favourite hotel every year, for both business and pleasure. Both native north-easterners, we now live 300 miles away in the Northumbrian countryside, but without that little bookshop and that very special venue, we would never have met.

When I proposed to Kathy she smiled at me and said: "Of all the people I served in the News Kiosk, you were the only one I didn't recognise". I can only say, thank heavens 007 didn't get there first!

EVEN THE VEG...
—— Celia Caliskan on a special place for mother and daughter.

The Royal Garden is my happy place. It is only associated with good memories. Having worked in Kensington for over 20 years I've had lots of celebrations in the Park Terrace Restaurant, in Bertie's Bar and at the 10th in the old days. These have included numerous birthdays, winning an award at work and even first dates.

I first came to the Royal Garden in the mid-1990s, when I came after work for drinks at the 10th when it was a Champagne Bar. I absolutely loved it from the first time I visited. I loved how civilised and peaceful it was, the staff were very polite and professional and the views were, and are, fantastic.

My happiest memories are those of taking my mum to lunch. As a fussy eater, who didn't really like vegetables, it was guaranteed that mum would clear her plate. She always remarked on how fresh and tasty the vegetables were. Coming from an era when all vegetables were boiled until they were soft and soggy, she didn't particularly like anything but peas. But at the Royal Garden she would eat all of the veg, especially French beans, mange tout and samphire. The dessert course was her favourite and mum's delight at being presented with such beautifully crafted creations really was the highlight of the meal. Mum could only manage small portions of any food but she always managed to eat the tuiles with the final coffee.

The hotel is so wonderful because of a combination of amazing service, friendly staff who make you feel special, a relaxed atmosphere and excellent, fresh, perfectly cooked, seasoned and presented food. Also, nowhere makes a dry martini as good as the Park Terrace!

SERVICE AND SMILES
—— Mair Barnes appreciates the thoughtfulness of the Royal Garden staff.

I have been staying at the hotel on and off for over 30 years – maybe even 40 years. In those early days the staff always greeted me warmly and used my business name – Barnes. Sometime in the early 1980s I was staying with my husband, whose surname is Read. As I walked to the reception the staff greeted me as Mrs Read. I was so impressed. That was so clever.

In the early 1980s I was a very frequent visitor as I was attempting to restore a large department store in Oxford Street to its former glory. I even stayed on Boxing Day a couple of times as I was casting my eye over trading on the first day of the sale in one of the stores for which I was responsible.

In April 2005, I was awarded a CBE for services to the Retail Sector and Business. The Queen was incredibly professional – it is amazing how she manages to remember to ask the relevant questions of the recipients of the various honours. I was very impressed when she asked me about working for the House of Fraser many years before.

I hosted a lunch on the top floor of the Royal Garden for my family and a few friends and it was lovely to admire the view from there. Both my mother and I received bouquets of flowers at the lunch. The hotel staff are so well trained and a special mention must go to Melissa, who rescued me two years ago when I needed help. I was on crutches and needed assistance to put on surgical stockings. Melissa persuaded a colleague to come and assist. What service!

Keep up the good work!

OF PEAS, DUCKS AND BASKETS

—— Sarah Woolmer looks back 50 years.

My first visit to the Royal Garden Hotel was at the end of 1966, after the World Cup. I went there to have a drink when I was a youngster from north Wales who'd just moved to London. My sister had announced she was moving to India and for some reason we ended up at the Royal Garden Hotel for a drink to say our farewell.

It may be 49 years ago but one thing that has really stuck in my mind is – and it's a ridiculous thing to remember – that a portion of petit pois, which was a new thing in those days, was 17 shillings and 6 pence, which would be the equivalent of 75p. Today that would be about £13! I remember saying that I'd never be able to afford to come here again!

But lo and behold, one way or another, I became a regular corporate customer in the late 1980s and I've been using the hotel ever since. I'm retired now but we used the Royal Garden for clients, and had regular conferences and sales meetings there, with our own VIPs coming in from all over the world as it's the right side of London for Heathrow. I know that when I was putting people into the Royal Garden – and some of them could be very fussy and very picky – that they'd look after them brilliantly, no matter how pernickety they were. They would always attend to all of my clients' needs.

Now I'm retired I'm still using the Royal Garden. I have an Executives' reunion lunch twice a year and when I suggested we use the Royal Garden they all said it's like coming home. They come in from Bangkok, Switzerland, Dubai and they'll all fly in just for lunch at the Royal Garden!

I've stayed there many times and I used to have two mementoes. In the executive rooms they used to have a very special plastic duck in each bathroom; it was red and white with a beak that went up and down. I was given one of those in about 1989 as part of a bag of goodies and I gave it to my granddaughter. Unfortunately – and I'm very cross with him – my son has recently thrown it away!

But I do still use a basket they had delivered to me one Christmas at work, which had freshly baked mince pies and lots of other goodies. That basket is still being used to this day in my bedroom, and it was used at my son and daughter-in-law's wedding, still with the same ribbons from the day I was given it. Although after losing my duck I'm not sure he deserved it!

MUSIC AND ROMANCE

—— **Angela Lambert on a special birthday.**

In 1973 I had my 21st birthday party at the Royal Garden Hotel with my two grandmothers, May Olive Williams and Olga Schröter, my parents, Keith and Lotte Williams, my sister, Kristina and my soon-to-be-fiance, Robert Lambert – he proposed to me that night after dinner.

Robert and I did a recce of several places in London for the dinner. We looked at the Savoy, the Dorchester, the Westbury and the Royal Garden. I had been to all those hotels before with my parents but we chose the Royal Garden because of the beautiful view, the music and the ambiance.

It was wonderful, full of atmosphere and we had a delicious dinner – with music from The Royal Roof Strings, which was a great memory – very romantic! I still have the Sydney Lipton LP that I bought on the evening.

TWO GIFTS IN ONE!
—— Isabelle Hart is full of thanks.

Thank you for my husband, Chaz, and thank you for introducing me to the wonderful music of John Wilson!

I worked as a children's eye surgeon at the Great Ormond Street Hospital and at almost 50 years of age I thought my patients over the years would be my only "family". My whole life changed when I attended a splendid dinner dance with friends one 5 November, ten years ago on the 10th floor of the Royal Garden Hotel.

Wow, what a view I had, especially all the fireworks! The band leader was John Wilson, who is now very well known, having conducted at the Last Night of the Proms, and I have loved his music since that night.

I chatted to a complete stranger while watching the fireworks and, yes, romance blossomed. After dining at separate tables he asked me to dance. As he is a professional musician – guitarist and composer – I was somewhat surprised he couldn't waltz but used the same foot twice every third step to stay in time with three-time!

I married Chaz two days before my 50th birthday and this year we celebrate our 10th wedding anniversary, so thank you Royal Garden Hotel!

WARDROBE MALFUNCTION!

—— **Diane Murphy says things don't always go to plan**.

I've been booking bands or staying at the Royal Garden for the last 20 years. My most recent stay still puts a smile on my face. Preparing for a series of rock and roll events, my room-mate Wendy Dio (wife of the late rock singer Ronnie James Dio) and I checked into our room at the hotel, unpacked our carefully chosen and well pressed outfits and hung them in the wardrobe. However, the weight of so much chic couture caused the rail to collapse, sending our finery into a heap on the floor.

A panicked call to the front desk sent a maintenance man scurrying to our rescue. Mission finally accomplished, all three of us were doubled up with laughter for quite a while!

It's my favourite hotel because of the amazing service, location, views, very professional staff, great food... oh, and kippers and Bloody Mary at breakfast!

THE MAGIC OF CHRISTMAS

—— Alan Place on a celebration to treasure.

Although we have stayed at the Royal Garden Hotel a number of times and enjoyed them all, the one that gave my wife Sylvia, my daughter Katrina and myself the most pleasure was over Christmas 2005.

We first stayed at the Royal Garden in celebration of Sylvia's 70th birthday in July of that year and it was a very special celebration for her. We then stayed again for Christmas 2005, which Sylvia says is one of the best Christmases of her life.

With the warmest welcome by the hotel's professional staff, together with the most wonderful huge basket of warm mince pies on the reception desk and the decorative tree on the edge of the Park Terrace Restaurant, we felt our perfect Christmas had truly begun.

On Christmas Eve we shopped in Harrods with our Christmas vouchers from our stay that were very much appreciated. We had an excellent lunch at the Georgian Restaurant at Harrods and imagine our surprise when we saw David and Victoria Beckham with their children and family and friends dining near to us in the restaurant. They had a large table in the centre and were just coming to the end of their meal as we were starting ours.

When we got back to our rooms after going to Carols by Candlelight at the Albert Hall, we found a fantastic presentation hamper filled with fruit, cake, mince pies, grapes and chocolates, all beautifully presented.

On Christmas Day we went to the 10th Restaurant for Christmas Lunch. There was a real festive atmosphere about the room and the tables were beautifully decorated with small marzipan figures and a tree. We sat by the windows overlooking Kensington Palace and Gardens. The staff were very attentive and friendly, the whole atmosphere with all the guests was relaxed and everybody seemed to enjoy themselves. Farther Christmas came round during the afternoon and distributed presents to all.

The food, needless to say, was superb; we still have the menu which was tied in a card showing the hotel in the snow. We also brought a little marzipan bear home and kept him as a lasting memory of our Christmas day.

The whole experience was magical. All the staff were very friendly and helpful and gave the hotel a feeling of warmth and homeliness. It was without doubt one of the best Christmases we have ever had.

ROOM WITH A VIEW

—— **Elizabeth Hurst enjoyed her wedding reception on the top floor of the Royal Garden in 1976.**

We were getting married at Christ Church, which is a nice, pretty church in Kensington. My husband Timothy lived nearby, and I had lived in Kensington but I'd gone off to work abroad in the Foreign Office. When I came back I bought a flat locally and we decided we wanted to get married in the area. We had a look at a famous hotel nearby and, because we didn't get married until our late 30s, they thought we were mother and father of the bride – which was lovely!

We decided we wanted to find somewhere with a view because weddings are always a bit of a nightmare as nobody knows each other – so we wanted them to at least be able to talk about the view if there was nothing else! And that was why we chose the Royal Garden – the view from the roof restaurant across Kensington Gardens was lovely. We managed to book the event for the afternoon, at about 3.30. We didn't go into the evenings in those days, so it was just the afternoon – it's only more recently that parents have had to cough up all of the money! We had just over 100 guests, which the roof restaurant easily accommodated. They had benches arranged down the side looking out at the view, and the guests thought it was fabulous – and luckily it wasn't raining.

We have wonderful memories and photos from the day, although the person who took the photographs at the reception forgot to put a filter on his lens and they all turned out rather pink! The hotel also gave us a copy of *Tatler* magazine, and inside was a piece on the hotel celebrating its 10th anniversary.

We've been back several times to the hotel and we're hoping to have our 40th anniversary celebrations there next April.

Dear Mr & Mrs Lajwii,

Wishing you a marvellous birthday together, and hope you might enjoy some of these wholefoods goodies during The Avengers this evening at the Odeon Lounge.

Happy Birthday!

Warm Regards,
Guest Relations.

A RINGING ENDORSEMENT

—— Brian Lajwii had an eventful stay.

My partner Katie and I had been together for six months when we decided to stay at the hotel for her birthday. I hadn't been to the hotel before but had heard about it and always planned to go there one day.

A few weeks prior to our stay I had bought an engagement ring. I knew the hotel would be the perfect setting as it always looked so amazing on the website and the reviews from guests were all brilliant. I also knew it would be perfect because Katie had always said she wouldn't enjoy it if I ever proposed to her in a public place such as a bar or restaurant, so a beautiful room overlooking Kensington Gardens would work very well.

We were both absolutely blown away by the level of service that we received from the moment that we arrived at the hotel. We felt like royalty and it just got better and better as our day progressed.

I was very nervous when we got to our room and concerned about the best moment to pop the question. Eventually Katie went to the bathroom and I quickly poured two glasses of champagne and waited around the corner on one knee. However, she was in the bathroom for a few minutes and my leg was beginning to cramp so I stood up to shake it off. She finally emerged and I fell to my knee again; she was very surprised to see me on one knee with a ring in my hand but also seemed to be in pain as she was clutching her finger. It turns out that while in the bathroom she had got her ring finger caught in the shower door!

Luckily, she said yes to my proposal but the ring didn't fit on her finger as it had started to swell! Eventually we managed to get the ring on and everything ended up OK!

We have returned to the hotel on quite a few occasions and the staff always go above and beyond to accommodate our requests. One time they allowed us to check in three hours early so that we could make our lunch reservation on the Thames and when we returned to the room we found chilled champagne and a hamper basket with a note from the Guest Relations team wishing us a happy birthday. It is without a doubt the greatest hotel we have ever stayed at and one that we will continue to visit for many years to come.

SIMPLY THE BEST

—— Keith and Eileen Davison-Pyott say only the Royal Garden will do.

When visiting London we have stayed at other hotels, but "our home" is without doubt the Royal Garden Hotel.

We have always loved staying at the Royal Garden, especially at Christmas and New Year. When the then 10th Restaurant was *the* place to be, we celebrated Christmas and New Year in style, and we have such fond memories of those perfect times in our lives.

We recently got married in London after being together for 26 years! We always said we would not get married unless we could do it in style, and only the Royal Garden Hotel could live up to our expectations. It was the best time ever, and our guests still talk about it with great memories of their stay at the hotel.

We have brought all of our children to the hotel over the years. They're now all grown up, and now we bring our grandchildren, who love visiting the hotel as much as we do. Whenever we mention to them that we are going to London they ask are we staying at the Royal Garden and can they come!

No other hotel in London can compare with the Royal Garden. They have it all: fantastic location, wonderful food, superb service, great management, and always a warm welcome. It is simply the best.

A LIFETIME OF MEMORIES

—— **Michael Harriman says the hotel keeps him and wife Judy youthful.**

After 40 years of marriage, the Royal Garden Hotel is part of us and we are part of it. They have adopted us. It's a very special hotel, it has a heart.

The team is a family and it is our home from home. We are looked after so well from the moment we arrive and it means the world to us. It keeps us interested in life.

The first time we went, we lived in Balham and I told Judy we were heading south to Bournemouth and it took her a while to realise I was driving north instead, because I was surprising her with a trip to the Royal Garden! We parked the car for £1 and had a fantastic time there.

Our careers took us away from London, but we retired around 1996 and bought a place a few minutes' walk from the hotel. We are very keen on music, met John Wilson, who would conduct and play at the hotel's Manhattan Nights once a month – fabulous memories!

I got ill, which slowed our pace of life. We came back every month to stay, and were looked after so well by the staff. We stay in a double-size room, number 815. It wasn't until we looked at the receipt for our honeymoon that we realised it was the same one!

During the Olympics a bloke wouldn't get out of 815. The hotel was very, very full except for the Royal Suite so we had that and invited plenty of our friends round. Elton John's chiropractor knocked on the door saying it was his room but we weren't going anywhere!

Everybody at the hotel has the same approach, a smile on welcome and they really look after you. When we have breakfast the room has always been done on our return so I can lie down, which is very important to me with my illness. It is the hotel which keeps us young.

GENERATION GAME
—— **It's fair to say that Khalifa Dasmal is no stranger to the Royal Garden Hotel.**

Khalifa first came over some 30 years ago with Sheikh Ahmed al Maktoum – a regular summer resident who loved the hotel so much that he nearly bought it in the late 1980s – and still uses it as his base during the flat racing season, calling the Royal Garden home from early summer to late autumn.

Khalifa says: "I love it here. Visitors from the Middle East are creatures of habit and we like to see the same trusted faces. Here at the Royal Garden we have got to know the management team and the Middle East Director Paul Sur and this makes the place feel like home. The service is excellent and the staff are friendly, accommodating and well-trained across the board – from room service to management. Most of my friends stay here for these reasons."

Paul Sur, who started out as a cashier at the Royal Garden 40 years ago, adds: "In the 1970s under James Brown the hotel made a concerted effort to attract visitors from the Middle East and ensured that they were catered for culturally. We are now seeing the fourth generation of the same families coming to the hotel. Trust and loyalty are everything. Middle Eastern visitors get used to individual members of staff – for example several guests who might have been coming here 20 or 30 years will simply not have the hotel's number but will call me direct instead. It's all about service, friendliness and patience. If something cannot be done, you make that clear, and when you do say yes, you can do something, you make absolutely sure it happens."

Khalifa has many great memories of times at the hotel: "I remember an incredible party in 1988 when Sheikh Ahmed's horse Mtoto won the King George VI and Queen Elizabeth Stakes, a fabulous night. And then my horse, Shaamit, trained by William Haggas and with Michael Hills on board, won the Derby in 1996. As the owner, I was taken to meet the Queen, who has famously never won the Derby [horses owned by the Queen have won over 1,600 races, including all five of the Classics except the Derby] and she told me how lucky I was to have a Derby winner when I owned so few horses!"

AND THE WINNER IS…

—— Lisa Osman recalls an awards ceremony.

My first memory of the stunning Royal Garden Hotel was attending the Great Taste Awards in 2013, where I was a judge. I absolutely loved the location, and felt very excited to be staying at the hotel and attending the awards. The fabulous meal created by the chefs – led by Steve Munkley – was simply outstanding.

Then the awards itself – truly the Oscars of the food world. The winner that year was Marybelle Dairy in Suffolk, a family-run business but on this occasion Katherine Strachan attended on her own.

The business was named after two of their original cows Mary and Belle. Once Katherine had scooped the regional award she was clearly totally overwhelmed and wanted to make her apologies to her fellow guests and leave to catch her train. Tortie Farrand from the Guild Of Fine Food thought she would have to hide Katherine's handbag to make sure that she didn't leave and miss her even bigger moment!

Then the drum roll, the lights and the film clips and Marybelle was the overall winner – the Supreme Champion of 2013! I had a lump in my throat as Katherine collected her award. A family business that had reached the top through sheer hard work and determination. Katherine said that the award would make the last 10 years worthwhile and the Royal Garden Hotel was the perfect location for such a remarkable and deserved award.

PERFECT VIEW

—— **Victoria Nother on Poppy's first birthday.**

John and I had the most amazing weekend at the Royal Garden to celebrate my daughter's first birthday! The staff were fantastic, the service was unbeatable and our room was gorgeous!

We chose the Royal Garden Hotel because of the reviews we read before booking and how welcome children seemed to be. Also the access to the hotel was close to a tube stop and the porters were more than happy to help with our pushchair and luggage and do anything to make life easy. The reviews lived up to expectations and with the park just next door our daughter Poppy gave it a big thumbs up.

She also loved the bear given to her on check-in, and she still has it in her cot. We've called it Bob as it was the only sound she could make at the time which sounded anything like a name!

Poppy was so obsessed with standing and looking out of the room across the park and we will now return every year to mark the occasion because we enjoyed it so much!

40 YEARS AND COUNTING
—— Andrea Morgale remembers good times.

On 10 June 1973, David and I had our wedding reception at the Royal Garden Hotel. Despite being the only day it rained during a heatwave, it was a marvellous day.

It was my parents (well, my mother!) who made the choice of venue. They chose it because of a combination of the size of the ballroom (we have a LOT of relatives), the high quality of the catering and the convenience of the location, both for Londoners and out-of-towners, most of whom stayed at the hotel for the weekend.

There are so many great memories from the day: being called "Mrs Morgale" for the first time when we arrived at the hotel after the ceremony, the festive atmosphere during the whole afternoon and evening, the arrangement and decoration of the ballroom and reception room, which were fabulous, and ending the evening with room-service of champagne and sandwiches with our closest friends in our lovely suite (having been too nervous to eat much of the lovely dinner!).

I remember one amusing incident. My brother had taken our luggage to the hotel for us on the morning of the wedding, and he decided to leave a bottle of champagne in our suite. He realised he should keep it cold, but wasn't sure how best to do this (he was very young!) so decided the best place was to fill the bidet in the bathroom with cold water and put it in there. The following morning, after enjoying a [lukewarm] bucks fizz with our room-service breakfast, we discovered the fully equipped fridge in the sitting room!

It was such a wonderful day that 40 years later we decided to go back to where it all began and hold our ruby wedding anniversary party there. This time, the sun shone brilliantly, matching our mood.

Fittingly, the private room of the Park Terrace Restaurant is designed for 40 people, so we had an amazing Sunday lunch there as well as a champagne reception in Bertie's Bar. Sadly, none of our parents are still alive, but our bridesmaid and best man were among the group of family and old friends who helped us celebrate, many of whom attended our wedding 40 years earlier.

We are now planning for 2023....

GROWING UP WITH THE HOTEL

—— Dennis McLaughlin goes back to where it all began.

The Royal Garden Hotel is a very special place to my wife and I as this year on 5 June we celebrated our 50th wedding anniversary.

My lovely wife Christine and I met in Kensington Gardens in summer 1964 inside the entrance to the left-hand side of the hotel. I was working on the construction of the hotel as a 17-year-old and Christine was working in the accounts department at Woolworths offices in Old Court Place Kensington.

Our relationship blossomed as we met every lunchtime and would stroll around Kensington Gardens watching the construction and progress in the building of the hotel.

Working on the hotel was a very happy period in my life as my parents divorced when I was six, and then my mother died when I was 10. This meant that my brother, sister and I were split up and sent to different children's homes. The joy of meeting my lovely wife in 1964

opened up a new and happy chapter for me, and the Royal Garden Hotel had a big part to play in this fortunate turn of events.

My wife and I stayed at the hotel in 2008 to celebrate our 43rd wedding anniversary. The staff were thrilled to hear that we had met there in 1964, so we have nothing but fond memories of the hotel. We were also there on 30 July, 1966 – the day England won the World Cup and when the team had their reception in the luxurious setting. Much to our delight we were standing outside when the team came out onto the balcony at the front of the hotel to acknowledge our cheers. What a happy, memorable time for us all.

Next year Christine and I will be 70 years old and we intend to have a celebration at the hotel with the theme "from 17 to 70 happy years" all due to the Royal Garden Hotel, which will stay in our hearts for ever.

FOOD & DRINK

———

Whether it's a black-tie banquet or a black coffee, the Royal Garden Hotel's commitment to five-star service has always been epitomised by the food and drink enjoyed by hundreds of guests every day

lawless fine dining is essential to the success of every five-star hotel. The story of food and drink at the Royal Garden is not, however, merely a half-century of haute cuisine and while the hotel can boast a rich history of classic French cooking and technical expertise, it is the breadth of dining options, an innovative, progressive approach to catering for the five-star market, and the standard of service that has been most remarkable over the years.

Three years before *Time Out* magazine's inaugural issue, *What's On In London* was already shaping the social and cultural lives of many Londoners. Their 'Good Food' column paid an early visit to the hotel in November 1965 and reported on the "very diverse restaurants under the Royal's roof". In the proceeding 50 years, the Royal Garden's food and beverage has continued to expand and modernise.

As well as great-tasting food, the hotel's menus have consistently been designed with value for money in mind, a fact that reflects the needs of the Royal Garden's eclectic clientèle. Similarly, whether it's a business guest in need of an early breakfast or a band looking for a post-performance nightcap, the hotel has always prided itself on keeping guests fed and watered whatever the time of day.

Celebrity chefs are almost de rigueur in the world of five-star hotels these days, but by resisting the temptation to follow this trend, the Royal Garden has put food before fame. Despite this, the hotel has attracted some of the world's most talented and respected chefs.

From Rémy Fougère (more on whom later) to John Williams (now Executive Chef at the Ritz) to David Nicholls (winner of two Michelin stars and many other industry accolades) to current Executive Head Chef Steve Munkley, the Royal Garden's brigade has been led by a series of talented and dedicated individuals.

Under the stewardship of these fantastic chefs, the Royal Garden Hotel has long been one of the most successful training grounds for the next generation of talent and today the hotel offers one of the biggest and most successful apprenticeship schemes in the UK.

Notable alumni of the Royal Garden include Paul Gayler (since worked at the Dorchester, Inigo Jones and the Lanesborough), Tony Love (the Grosvenor), David Marshall (the Athanaeum) and Clinton Lovell (the Ritz) to name but a few.

Elsewhere in this book you will find plenty of stories pertaining to the more famous and flamboyant individuals to have walked through the lobby of the Royal Garden Hotel over the last 50 years, but some of the most spectacular food produced during this time has been of the mass-catered-for-variety – for dinners, concerts and awards ceremonies in the hotel's banqueting and conference suites. In fact, at present, conference and

banqueting accounts for around 35 per cent of all the food and drink at the hotel, a reflection of the Royal Garden's credentials as a leading hotel for business travellers and one of London's premier events providers.

Despite catering for many corporate diners, the hotel is equally well set up to serve the needs of those who call Kensington home and many locals are regular visitors to the Park Terrace restaurant, bar and lounge, while the Maze Coffee House, situated where Bodo's is today, was a big hit with passing trade in the hotel's early days.

Across the lobby, Bertie's Bar (and its previous incarnations) makes everyone – from Kensington residents to long-lost travellers – feel like locals. The man behind this special atmosphere, and a member of staff at the Royal Garden for 45 years, was Luis Cobas. Luis sadly passed away in June 2015, but his legacy of warm service and care for all customers remains a benchmark for the hotel's front-of-house teams.

Of course, fine dining has always been and remains a major calling card for the hotel and Min Jiang, the latest re-imagining of the impressive tenth floor restaurant space, reflects the hotel's forward-thinking attitude. A destination restaurant for residents and London foodies alike, this modern Chinese restaurant offers dramatic views, a bold, stylised dining room, and highly original Oriental cuisine. The transformation of this stunning venue over the past 50 years sums up the Royal Garden's bold approach to the twin aims of exciting and satisfying guests at the dinner table.

FOOD FOR EVERY OCCASION

When the Royal Garden opened in 1965, its restaurants were quick to gain critical acclaim. One of the first visitors to the hotel's original four restaurants was 'What's On in London's' Good Food column.

MAZE COFFEE HOUSE

as described in *What's On In London*, November 18, 1965

Cheapest of the four [restaurants in the hotel], well within anyone's purse, is MAZE COFFEE HOUSE, on the lower ground floor, which opens 24 hours of every 24 – which simply means that it never shuts – offers simple fare like Smoked Salmon (7s. 6d.), Fried Fillet of Sole (5s. 6d.), Turkey Sandwiches (3s. 6d.) and Peach Melba (3s.).

Breakfast here can be had for a few shillings (Tea, Toast or Croissant and Marmalade will cost you only 3s. 6d.). Tea with assorted Danish or French pastries is little more, and for 10s. you could have a small feast.

The present Maze menu, by the way, is a temporary one; soon a more elaborate one will come into force which will offer a wide variety of food for every occasion from Iced Melon (2s.), Hot Onion Flan (2s.) and Sole and Scampi grilled on a skewer (6s 6d.) through Omelettes, Sandwiches and Pancakes to Orange Freeze and other soda fountain fantasies.

THE BULLDOG BAR AND CHOPHOUSE

as described in *What's On In London*, November 18, 1965.

There isn't a large menu here, but it is a mouth-watering one. Avocado Pear is offered as an appetiser (6s.), with the alternative of Game Pâtés, Galantines or Charcuterie on display; or there are a couple of soups: Crème du Jour or Consommé du Jour (3s).

Steaks here vary between 14s. and 18s., but lamb chops, pork chops, chump chops and chicken from the spit are less expensive alternatives. And you might like to try the Bulldog's great speciality, the Steak and Kidney Pie (17s. 6d.). Included in these prices, by the way, are potatoes and salad.

Integral in this [oaky, masculine] restaurant is the Oyster Bar. Sweets or cheese; and a good wine list and beers.

THE ROYAL ROOF
as described in *What's On In London*, November 26, 1965

But maybe you want a truly memorable evening? ...The Bar [in the Royal Roof Restaurant] opens at 7.30 so you can sip your aperitif as you look out over the twinkling lights of London. Dinner is served from 8.30 p.m. and you have the word of a Frenchman, a gourmet, that this is the kind of dinner which is normally the prerogative of only the top-flight French Parisian restaurant.

Towering into the Kensington sky, the Royal Garden is a London landmark; it is a Good Food landmark, too, for there aren't many hotels in London that can offer such diverse kinds of Eating Out under the one roof or the epicurean perfection of the Royal Roof.

What's On In London, November 1965

THE GARDEN ROOM
as described in *What's On In London*, November 26, 1965

This week… we're taking you up in the world to report on the really beautiful, sunny GARDEN ROOM, the long, high-ceilinged restaurant which looks out across Kensington Gardens and the Palace.

The prices here are just about the level of any top-class restaurant in town… And really unusual value is offered here by the 25s. three-course table d'hôte lunch and four-course dinner.

The beautifully set-out à la carte menu here offers plenty of exploration opportunities for the gourmet. Foie Gras from Strasbourg will cost you half a guinea, but it is perfect.

[You] get good value here: there's spaciousness between tables, the impeccable service… the lovely view – and the surrounding celebrities.

Congratulations on your 50th anniversary.
          Many Happy Returns.

The Maze Story – fifty years on.

Some memories are so pleasant and vivid that five decades later they are as fresh as ever. The waft of hot chocolate and Danish pastries in a most congenial setting, the Maze, belongs to those memories. After a run through Hyde Park and Kensington Gardens where our two young children would float their mini sailboat and feed the swans, the Maze was the venue of choice for a special treat. The Maze had its own entrance – now the Royal Garden Hotel Night Club's – then down a ramp leading to the lower ground floor, the colour scheme dark brown wood and avocado. The "in", height of fashion in those days, arranged in a kind of labyrinth. The enclosed festooned paper table mat with its maze pattern goes back to those days. Pencil tracing the path to the centre of the maze kept young and old thoroughly amused. In our family The Maze Treat became an almost weekly tradition. Happy days indeed. Although we have swapped the lower ground floor – the Maze having long gone – for the 10th floor and its Chinese Restaurant, delicious and sophisticated, we recall with nostalgia the Amazing Maze days of yore.

                With best wishes,
                Anne & Allen (the)

12th February 2015

Regular visitors to Maze (and now Min Jiang), Anne and Allen wrote to congratulate the Royal Garden on reaching the Big 5-0, and share some happy memories from regular family visits to the hotel's coffee house half a century ago.

A choice of excellent restaurants and bars

On the tenth floor, the Royal Roof Restaurant combines the most spectacular views of London's skyline with some of the finest cuisine in the city. Here you can enjoy a tranquil breakfast, reasonably priced lunch or a sumptuous dinner, with dancing until 1am at the weekend. On the ground floor, the Garden Café offers all-day dining. It has a beautiful view across the Park through picture windows, as does the nearby Garden Bar, which is a lively meeting place where you can listen to our resident pianist whilst trying one of our exotic cocktails. In contrast, the Gallery Bar, overlooking the foyer and Kensington High Street, combines the comfortable surroundings of a gentlemen's club with a wine-bar style menu.

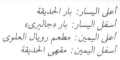

Top Left: Garden Bar
Above: Gallery Bar
Top Right: Royal Roof Restaurant
Bottom Right: Garden Café

أعلى اليسار: بار الحديقة
أسفل اليسار: بار «جاليري»
أعلى اليمين: مطعم رويال العلوي
أسفل اليمين: مقهى الحديقة

上段左：ガーデン・バー
下段左：ギャラリー・バー
上段右：ロイヤル・ルーフ・レストラン
下段右：ガーデン・カフェ

An early promotional brochure showcasing the range of dining options available to the Royal Garden's guests.

IN THE GARDEN

The Garden Café and Garden Bar, later transformed into the Park Terrace, was a bistro and lounge bar widely used by residents and locals alike. This promotional shot from the 1980s shows that the Royal Garden's commitment to both comfort and style is nothing new.

Located on the ground floor of the hotel, a short walk from the main reception, the Park Terrace has been totally transformed since its days as the Garden Café and Bar. The modern and, in many ways, now minimalist restaurant, bar and lounge is used for breakfast, morning coffee, relaxed meetings, afternoon tea and as a venue for under-stated but sophisticated modern British dining.

The Park Terrace is open to guests 365 days a year; it's the boiler house of food and drink in the hotel. We pride ourselves in maintaining our five-star standards every single day – ruin the last morning of someone's stay with a bad breakfast and the whole stay is ruined.

Jonathan Lowrey, General Manager, Royal Garden Hotel

The Park Terrace is one of London's most popular places to take afternoon tea. Over the years there have been some impressive creations sent to the table.

A spectacular afternoon tea served at the Park Terrace in 2012 to celebrate the Queen's diamond jubilee.

A ROOM WITH A VIEW

The hotel's most dramatic dining space, the tenth and top floor of the Royal Garden, has been home to three different fine dining restaurants – the Royal Roof, The Tenth and, since 2008, Min Jiang.

The hotel's original tenth floor restaurant, the Royal Roof served first-class French food until the hotel's refurbishment in the '90s.

THE HEIGHT OF GOOD TASTE

The Royal Garden Hotel has boasted many high-flying staff over the years, but none more so than the chef precariously suspended outside the Royal Roof in these promotional shots from the 1980s.

Our intrepid hero may not be fully appreciating the fantastic vistas of Kensington Gardens and Hyde Park, but these peerless views have played a major part in the enduring appeal of the hotel's tenth floor restaurants.

TALK OF THE TOWN

Dim Sum, spicy Sichuan dishes and Beijing duck are the signature dishes at Min Jiang. The highly skilled and time-consuming processes involved in the preparation of these and other items sees the relatively small kitchen on the tenth floor house 22 cooks.

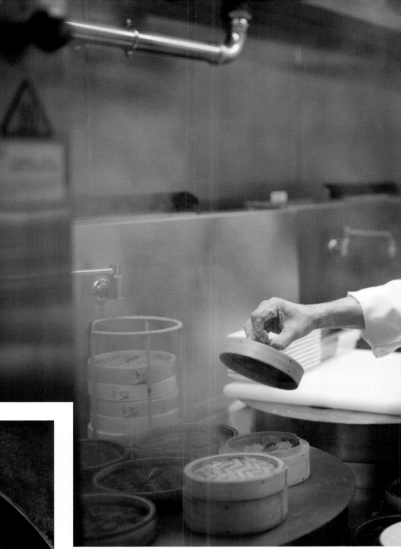

When our chef started at Min Jiang, we laid out 20 ducks for him to choose from. He cooked them all and said none of them were good enough to serve. Fortunately we found an alternative!
Steve Munkley, Executive Head Chef at the Royal Garden Hotel

WELL OILED MACHINE

Servicing almost 400 guest rooms, walk-in customers, conferences and banquets, the Royal Garden's biggest challenge has always been to maintain the highest of standards while catering for the masses.

Over the years, innovations such as pantries on every floor of the hotel (no longer in service) and a state-of-the-art banqueting kitchen have helped the Royal Garden live up to its five-star status, while the main kitchen was fully refurbished in 2014.

Chef de cuisine Rémy Fougère oversees another banquet.

Executive Head Chef Steve Munkley on some of the many events he has overseen since joining as Executive Chef in 1996…

The opening of the hotel in 1996 following the major refurbishment was pretty spectacular. We had food offerings all the way around the building: a boat in the Park Terrace filled with ice and a huge seafood display and our Pastry Chef made an incredible chocolate presentation.

Industry dinners are always great fun, and within a year of opening I was doing The Craft Guild of Chefs awards dinner – that's 350 chefs coming to the hotel, to eat food created by the new kid on the block!

Conferences can be even bigger. The International Live Music Conference is a huge event every year. For a whole weekend in March, they take over the hotel – there are about 700 people. That one's a lot of fun.

We also do plenty outside of the hotel as well. We've been at Kensington Palace with the Royal College of Music, at the Holland Park Opera, and a few years ago we took Min Jiang to Taste of London.

The state-of-the-art Palace Suite
dressed for dinner.

The 38th
Pathfinder Ball

ROYAL GARDEN HOTEL
KENSINGTON, LONDON, W.8

DECEMBER 6th, 1980

The Royal Celebration Ball
(in aid of the Muscular Dystrophy Charity)

Royal Garden Hotel
Kensington

Wednesday, 29th July, 1981

THE FOOTBALL ASSOCIATION

1981

100

Celebration Banquet

Watching banquet service at the
Royal Garden Hotel… is like watching
a carefully choreographed show.

The Caterer and Hotelkeeper, 1981

FOOD AS ART

The hotel underwent a full kitchen renovation in early 2014, with the entire main kitchen equipped with state-of-the-art, eco-friendly appliances. The project saw a brand new floor laid, with a non-slip resin applied to it, and the installation of new ceilings and walls containing hygienic, easy-to-clean "Whiterock". The kitchen uses induction cooking, which means that heat transfer only happens when a pot is placed on a stove.

Bertie's Bar was transformed for the 2015 Rugby World Cup.

CHEERS!

Bertie's Bar, and previously The Gallery, has served a variety of purposes over the past 50 years. As a meeting place for a pre-dinner or late-night drink, the mezzanine location has offered both convenience and privacy for guests arriving at the hotel or heading off for a night on the town. It has also been the focal point for many a sports team's post-match celebrations. On a more functional level, it is used for business events, press conferences and as a discreet meeting space.

To many, the history of the bars at the Royal Garden Hotel will be inextricably tied up with a fabulous 30-year partnership between Luis Cobas and Manuel Rebon. The two compañeros were an integral part of the hotel's warm and welcoming service until Manuel's retirement in 2013 and Luis's untimely death in 2015. They set an exceptionally high standard for the many bar staff they mentored and worked alongside.

Where there's fine dining there's fine wine. Cellarmen at the Royal Garden in 1967 show off a double-magnum of rare claret, part of the hotel's impressive collection for connoisseurs.

139

Royal Garden Hat-Trick

For the third year running and for the fourth time in five years, the Royal Garden's Darts Team have won First Division of the Inner London Hotel and Catering Darts League.

However, this year they have beaten even that record by also winning the Watney's Knockout Championships.

Altogether this year, they collected sixteen cups and trophies.

Seen with all their "silver" are left to right: Mark French, Larder Chef; Joe Dinn, Banqueting Electrician; Charlie Putt, Head Luggage Porter; Ted Tree, (Captain), Painter; Ron Painter, Shift Engineer and Clinton Lovell, Larder Chef.

BEHIND THE SCENES

Behind the pristine plates of food served up at the Royal Garden Hotel are countless stories of callow chefs finding their feet at one of the most prestigious kitchens in Great Britain. Now the owner of the Romney Bay House Hotel in Kent, Clinton Lovell remembers the "interesting" welcome and the rewarding way of life that he enjoyed at the Royal Garden when he arrived as a fresh-faced teenager in the late '70s...

I had an interview with Rémy [Fougère] on a Friday afternoon. It must have been the shortest interview of all time. He asked me why I wanted to be a chef, I said something along the lines of "I've got a real passion and interest etc. etc.", and he said "Okay, when can you start?". I had just finished my first year of college, I was only 16, but he said he wanted me in the following morning at 7am. He didn't give me any more details, but I assumed we'd work everything out later.

When I arrived, I was sent to sit in the changing rooms and three lads came in and sorted me out with whites from the linen room, but when I walked into the kitchen I met Paul [Executive Sous Chef, Paul Gayler] and he said: "Who the f*ck are you?". I told him I was starting today. "Well, f*cking nobody's told me!" It was an interesting way to start your first day at work and when personnel got wind of it they weren't best pleased, particularly as they had to find me a place to live in the hostel round the corner! But that's the way chefs were in those days – not too keen on paperwork!

I really enjoyed life in the hostel. It was pretty basic, with communal wash areas, but not being mollycoddled really did set you up for the pressure of the kitchen and for the rest of your life. And it was the first chance for a lot of us to get away from our parents and actually stand on our own two feet. We had guys from all over the country coming together and living in that place created a real bond.

A lot of us were involved with the social club at the hotel too. We had a darts team and I started a fishing club. It was a way to integrate everyone in the hotel, and meet the guys – in maintenance, the electricians, the banqueting team – who we didn't see much of during the working day. We worked hard, but we also had a lot of fun.

LOOKING EAST

Over the years, the hotel has become a popular choice with many Middle Eastern guests and special menus have been designed to reflect their dietary requirements and cultural traditions, including daytime fasting during Ramadan.

Despite this careful planning, not everything always goes to plan as Paul Gayler, Executive Sous Chef at the Royal Garden from 1975-1980, remembers: "We had some crazy requests sometimes. You'd get an order through for 10 whole lambs, then the next day, another guest would say, "How many did he have? 10? We'll have 11". It was madness – we'd be sending up these huge bits of meat, plus 40 or 50 poussins. I remember once, we sent up an order like this, then it came back down about 10 minutes later with a message: 'They've changed their mind chef, they're going out for dinner'."

Rémy Fougère of the Royal Garden

KING OF THE KITCHEN

Respected and feared in equal measure, Rémy Fougère oversaw the Royal Garden's kitchen between 1972 and 1989, and led the way in establishing the quality of the hotel's cuisine.

Surprisingly, especially given his appearance – the very model of a Gallic chef – Fougère never intended to end up in a kitchen ("I thought I might be a mechanical engineer" he told *The Caterer & Hotelkeeper* in 1981), yet ended up overseeing the Royal Garden's brigade of cooks for the best part of two decades.

Hailing from Saint-Jean-d'Angély in south-western France, Fougère learned his trade travelling the world but settled in England for good in 1972 having married his wife Josephine in Manchester, and soon set to work creating an incredible legacy at the Royal Garden Hotel.

Steve Munkley, Executive Head Chef at the Royal Garden Hotel remembers: "Rémy used to do a lot of shooting and he used to bring carloads of pheasants back on Monday morning. He was a great chap to work for – I was a young Commis Chef at the time and the Royal Garden was very much a training ground for young chefs in London."

Paul Gayler once let the following slip: "He could lift a cook by his toggle with one hand, and hold him an inch from the kitchen floor… One day he was tasting a sauce I'd made and suddenly he hit me, whack, right under the rib cage, and I doubled up in pain. I thought I was dying. When I looked up he was smiling: 'Not bad for an Englishman'."

And finally, John Williams, who was Chef at the hotel from 1976-85, told the caterer.com in 2013: "Coming to the Royal Garden Hotel was the real start of my career. The chef there was Rémy Fougère and he really developed me. He was a good teacher: he would take me to France and show me all kinds of great restaurants."

Things go pretty smoothly here on the whole. There is seldom a lot of fuss or yelling. When chefs lose their temper, it's usually because they are not doing their own job properly. When I do lose my temper it's usually premeditated, because I think the fellow needs that sort of emotional shock to shake him out of his lethargy.

Rémy Fougère, speaking to The Caterer & Hotelkeeper in 1981

NEW ORDER

Appointed during the major re-development of the hotel in the 1990s, Executive Head Chef Steve Munkley, alongside a fantastic team of chefs, has – quite literally – taken the Royal Garden's food into the 21st century. The Park Terrace has become a two-rosette restaurant, while Min Jiang, with three rosettes of its own, is a destination restaurant in the capital's dining scene.

The extensive team's passion for good food and quality produce is matched by the hotel's passion for staff development and training, with a commitment to excellence keeping the Royal Garden at the forefront of both fine dining and industry practice.

Steve says: "I'd been at the hotel as a Commis Chef in the early '80s, so I knew the place, and knew what was

possible in the building. I got a call from a friend telling me the job was up for grabs. I came in for an interview with the General Manager and luckily enough I convinced him that the man he'd initially chosen for the job wasn't the right one and that I should be doing it instead!

"It was important for me that there was an Executive Chef overseeing everything. In a place like this, you couldn't have separate people in charge of separate outlets, because there's a big crossover – with what is bought and used, where stuff is stored, how events are catered for etc. We are one place, so we have to work as one."

What the team of chefs offer to guests is huge variety and that is also what they get in their day-to-day working environment. One minute it's an awards dinner for 400 people, the next it's sending up pizzas with room service. They always seem to cope, even when situations are thrown at them such as an airport closure meaning 300 guests unexpectedly staying on, and every one of them vegetarian!

STAFF

Without its staff – loyal, dedicated
and skilled – a hotel is nothing.
The Royal Garden is no different

Members of staff go about their business while the executive team sets the hotel's strategy during a weekly meeting.

The Royal Garden Hotel has always prided itself on its people – the way it looks after them, their friendliness and willingness to go the extra mile to make the guest experience as good as it can be. With over 40 languages spoken by staff within the hotel, and upwards of 50 nationalities, this is a complex operation and a lot of care and attention is put into ensuring staff have everything they need to do the job to the best of their ability.

Talking to the large number of Royal Garden employees who have been here for more than ten years, many of them substantially longer, the refrain is the same – the hotel feels like a family, people look out for each other, they enjoy each other's company, and everybody shares the ethos that if you are going to provide guests with the best possible service, it helps if you feel the same about your employment – that you are respected, trusted and supported. Do as you would be done by, the saying goes.

Training in a number of roles within the hotel is another common theme among the staff – in a family, however good the preparation, sometimes things don't go exactly to plan and everyone has to muck in, so knowing the ropes is vitally important.

And the talk of a family atmosphere is not simply a construct set up to provide a point of differentiation. Long service awards at the Royal Garden are unusual in the hotel industry for the number of people, especially senior staff who set the tone, who are being recognised for their service over 10, 15, 20, and in some cases 30 years.

Tellingly, guests recognise and appreciate the hotel's staff. Whether it be returning honeymooners, sporting teams back in London to do battle once more, or stars of stage or screen returning to their favourite bolt hole in the capital, the number who cite the friendliness and professionalism of the staff as a key factor in the enjoyment of their stay is staggering. Whether it be on arrival, in the bars and restaurants, for room service, or in management, a friendly and recognisable face makes guests feel right at home.

General Manager Jonathan Lowrey, who himself has been with the hotel for 20 years, says: "The intention is really to emphasise what makes the Royal Garden Hotel stand out as a five-star hotel. That has always been down to a heavy focus on a team of staff who are flexible and genuinely interested and want to deliver top-quality customer service. We are a family business, having had so many people live and work together for a decade and more."

Lowrey may well have added: "More than 250 of our people have been with us for over five years and most of the key managers for over ten. I believe the cornerstone of a successful hotel is happy, communicative staff. Training is vital and continuous, the only way you can get commitment," but in fact these words were spoken by then General Manager James Brown, back in 1988. An illustration, if one were needed, that the commitment to staff development is not a recent idea.

Over the following pages, we talk to a few of today's staff about the hotel and their experiences of working there, and celebrate the life of one member of staff who for many, epitomised everything that is good about the hotel.

SIMPLY THE BEST

The hotel's legendary Bar Manager Luis Cobas, the heartbeat of the hotel, passed away at the start of June 2015.

The outpouring of love and grief from staff and guests alike showed just how much of a part of people's lives Luis had become and the regard in which he was held.

Luis was a much-loved colleague, bringing character, warmth and personality to the hotel and genuinely caring about guests. Born in Lugo in Spain, he came to the UK in the late 1960s and joined the Royal Garden in 1970. Starting in the Royal Roof Restaurant as a Commis Waiter, he learnt the art of service excellence and was soon offered a job in the Bulldog Bar and Chophouse. He worked there for 12 years before transferring to the Lobby Bar in the hotel then the Gallery Bar (now Bertie's Bar).

In 1996, as the hotel opened after refurbishment, Luis received an offer from newly appointed General Manager Graham Bamford, who asked him if he "wanted his bar back". Luis readily accepted and returned as Bar Manager of the newly named Bertie's Bar.

His career as a Bar Manager saw him care for countless guests, including the many celebrities and other high-profile individuals who frequent the hotel. His gentle, kind and friendly nature meant he was a hugely popular and trusted figure, amongst staff and guests alike, always offering superlative service.

He believed that working in a bar is not just about serving drinks and he always went the extra mile, finding out from guests the purpose of their visit and their likes and dislikes. He was famous for remembering each guest's favourite tipple and his advice to his team was: "Try your hardest, be fair, be loyal, and then you will get your reward." He will be sadly missed.

SERVICE WITH A SMILE

Room Service Manager Giovanni Gargasole tells a not atypical story of coming over to the UK – in his case in 2002 from Italy, where he studied economics – and being taken on while he learnt English, enjoying the family atmosphere of the hotel, being challenged, and thriving. Like many members of staff at the hotel, Giovanni has worked in numerous positions, giving him a broad understanding of the workings of the Royal Garden.

He says: "You have to deal with different personalities, different characters, people with different backgrounds and different expectations. It's a great learning experience and you have the opportunity to mould people into the Royal Garden way of doing things. We help each other, we listen, and we expect the highest standards."

The hotel attracts its fair share of stars and the staff need to respond to their requests without treating them any differently from other guests. Giovanni says: "When Justin Bieber was in it was funny as he was underage and we therefore couldn't serve him any alcohol! And I remember Michael Jackson being here, as well as Oliver Stone and Bernardo Bertolucci. He was a hero of mine and we got chatting – it just so happened his brother had a place near my village in Puglia."

THE ART OF COMMUNICATION

Telephone and Business Centre Manager Sue Newland and her colleague Yolande McCourt have seen – and heard – it all in in their combined 40 years at the hotel. As communications systems have developed into the hi-tech operation they are today, Sue's and Yolande's roles have evolved.

Yolande says: "I think it's fair to say there was a bit of eavesdropping in the early days with the old doll's eye plug boards. Not by us of course! But these days it is all so different, so much faster and more efficient, and it changes so rapidly – we'll have another upgrade next year. A bit of the romance may have gone but for guests, it's so much better."

Yolande admits a lifelong obsession with the hotel – as a schoolgirl she bunked off to cheer on The Monkees here in the 60s and had an initial stint here working as a telephonist in the 70s as well. She remembers Michael Jackson calling down for crayons for his kids, Mike Yarwood staying for months on end, the "gorgeous" Julio Iglesias, Stevie Wonder, Cirque du Soleil, Keith Moon being a "typical rockstar", Tina Turner, Andrea Bocelli…

More recently, when teen sensation Justin Bieber stayed, he put out a message on Twitter saying where he was staying and the team subsequently had to field some 20,000 calls in four days, with callers "pretending to be this and that, saying they were his girlfriend and could we put them through… could I have his towels, can I clean his toilet…"

WEDDING BELLS

Reception Manager Felicity Myers is not the first, and probably not the last, Royal Garden Hotel employee to find romance within the hotel that has led to wedding bells, and she is also not the first to have had a range of roles within the hotel, including Guest Relations.

Felicity, another member of staff to start work here in the last century, says: "My sister was working here as a Pastry Chef and encouraged me to do the same and I've never looked back! I'd never been to London but came down as a 21-year-old and just loved it. I started as a Telephonist and have done a whole range of roles since then."

Felicity, along with other members of staff like Nina the Pianist and Luis the Bar Manager, looked after long-term resident Mrs Preece. Felicity says: "She used to come in every lunchtime with her husband and have a bowl

of chips and a glass of wine. He died about 12 years ago and she was lost without him so she sold her flat and possessions and basically moved in and lived here for 10 years. A bowl of chips at lunch, a glass or two of merlot in the evening, she'd listen to Nina play in the Park Terrace, go and have drink with Luis in Bertie's and she was very happy. Everybody knew her and she was just a part of the family. We even took her out for lunch when she'd been here for 10 years! When her health deteriorated, Mr Lowrey took her down to get registered with a doctor (he even got a parking ticket!) and made sure she was well looked after."

And what of the wedding? "4 January 2014. An amazing day. I ended up picking all the rooms for the guests because my now husband Martin had arranged everything else. It was exhausting but exhilarating."

OF SPORT AND SONG

Reservations and Groups Sales Executive Manager Gill Evans is another with a long history of working at the hotel, even penning many of the stories in the Rank Group's newsletters in the '80s. She remembers Oliver Reed staying – "despite his hell-raising reputation he was utterly charming, full of brilliant stories and still with a glint of danger in his eyes!

"We have also had a host of musicians staying – it's near the record companies, near the agents, near the venues, so we always had popstars coming and going. They could stay slightly under the radar with us as well, with nobody in their face. Jim Kerr has been a regular for years, Elton John's band love it here, The Who, Michael Jackson, Chuck Berry – he was booked somewhere else, and he didn't like it so he came over here."

Gill recalls how sports stars became regular guests after the reopening in the mid-1990s, starting with being named UEFA headquarters for the 1996 Euros. "Before then we did have football teams regularly staying, and some of the tennis players used us during Wimbledon fortnight, but we really became renowned as the hotel for sportspeople from the late '90s and now we are regularly pitching for sporting business.

"It's great to have all the sports teams over and as so many of them travel with their families these days the atmosphere is brilliant. You'll find a touring party of 30 or so players can swell to more than double that with wives, girlfriends and children. With the 2015 Ashes touring group there was even a one-month-old! It makes things a bit more challenging having to arrange interconnecting rooms and making sure they've got all the right cots, beds, high chairs and the like but it's great fun and all part of our family-friendly philosophy."

STRIVING FOR PERFECTION

Alan Robinson, veteran of 18 years and now Operations Manager having previously been House Manager and Head Waiter, says: "I would say, compared to the rest of the hotels that I've worked at, this is the most family-orientated one."

Alan, who has had to deal with fires, floods and blizzards, has three memories that will stick with him. He says: "First up was when a guy lost his wife's ring in the bathroom sink on the day of the wedding! We got up there, took things apart, got it back from the u-bend, and returned it to its rightful owner. Panic over!

"Then we had the Virgin Atlantic balloon in the hotel when Branson was attempting to become the first man to circumnavigate the globe non-stop by balloon. They got the temperature as cold as they could to give them a feel for what it would be like and it was amazing....

"And another time during a conference a waiter walked onto a stage to give President Putin and the other delegates some water. I don't know if he realised they were filming but we all did and I was so embarrassed! Gave him a proper ticking off!

"Nine times out of ten guests would not even notice when things don't entirely go to plan. We beat ourselves up because we strive for perfection. Obviously it's not always achievable but it doesn't stop us trying."

THE NEXT 50 YEARS

—— **General Manager Jonathan Lowrey looks to the future.**

A Royal Garden Hotel employee for almost 20 years, Jonathan Lowrey has played a crucial role in the running and development of the Royal Garden Hotel over the past two decades and, along with the owners, has a clear vision for the future.

He explains: "We are justifiably proud of what we have achieved, which is reflected in the hotel's AA five red star status. We are all aware that the London hotel market is competitive and fast-moving and we are determined to maintain our distinctive quality of service and to continually improve our already high standards. Together with a team of staff who are motivated and dedicated, we look forward to the next 50 years!"

ACKNOWLEDGEMENTS

Thank you to everyone who has helped put this book together, particularly all of the staff and guests – past and present – at the Royal Garden Hotel, most notably Mark Anderson, Anita Benyon, Charlie Smallcombe and Alex Trebucq.

To Matt Thacker, Dan Brigham, Sam Stow and Juliette Kristensen for the research and writing.

To the Royal Borough of Kensington and Chelsea and Dave Walker for help with local history and images.

Photographs are from the hotel's own archives, from Getty Images (thanks to Tom Shaw and Karl Bridgeman) or from guests. We apologise in advance if there are any images whose copyright we have not successfully managed to track down.